Culture, Industrialisation and Education

Culture, Industrialisation and Education

by G. H. Bantock

Professor of Education,
University of Leicester

LONDON
ROUTLEDGE AND KEGAN PAUL
NEW YORK: HUMANITIES PRESS

First published 1968
by Routledge and Kegan Paul Ltd
Broadway House, 68–74 Carter Lane
London, E.C.4

Printed in Great Britain
by Cox & Wyman Limited
London, Fakenham and Reading

SBN 7100 6132 3 (c)
SBN 7100 6133 1 (p)

THE STUDENTS LIBRARY OF EDUCATION has been designed to meet the needs of students of Education at Colleges of Education and at University Institutes and Departments. It will also be valuable for practising teachers and educationists. The series takes full account of the latest developments in teacher-training and of new methods and approaches in education. Separate volumes will provide authoritative and up-to-date accounts of the topics within the major fields of sociology, philosophy and history of education, educational psychology, and method. Care has been taken that specialist topics are treated lucidly and usefully for the non-specialist reader. Altogether, the Students' Library of Education will provide a comprehensive introduction and guide to anyone concerned with the study of education and with educational theory and practice.

J. W. TIBBLE

In much that has been written about the Sociology of Education during the past decades, there has been an emphasis upon the contribution of education to social mobility, its instrumental role in a technological society, the way in which it reflects, reinforces and modifies social class and status differences. In *Culture, Industrialisation and Education* Professor Bantock takes a very different standpoint: His concern is with the cultural values that underlie the content of our educational provision, with the way in which industrialisation and the mass communication characteristic of advanced technology have affected what we try to do in schools and the way in which we do it. Professor Bantock argues that the traditional curriculum, with its stress upon cognative and intellectual processes, is in many cases irrelevant to the needs of the child whose future lies, not in academic pursuits, but in automated factory, farm and service occupation. Such a curriculum 'nowhere seriously touches those cultural experiences in terms of which a considerable majority are going to spend the rest of their lives'. At a time when we are trying to provide a fuller and longer secondary education, not just for a selected minority, but for the whole population, there are few issues more urgent and important than those discussed in this book.

WILLIAM TAYLOR

v

Contents

Every Group has to have a gimmick, even ones that haven't got as far as making an L.P. The Pineapple Truck's is that they are the group with the highest I.Q. in the country. They have two open exhibitioners and one open scholar. . . . All are first-year undergraduates at Cambridge. . . .

Some members of the group say they would have no hesitation about leaving if a good offer arrived. 'It's the first thing in life I've *really* been interested in,' says . . . the open scholar. 'I took it up out of general boredom with Cambridge, and it escalated. I'm not hung up on a degree or a respectable job. I think the whole of the pop scene, the poetry and the music, has much more relevance to life.'

Sunday Times, 14 May, 1967.

I see pop music and indeed pop art generally as a defiant relinquishing of responsibility towards the society, the responsibility of thinking, the responsibility of being committed to any idea, to any point of view, to any course of action; and it's this negative attitude to society, to human thought, to historical processes and all the rest of it which, it seems to me, permeates the whole of beat music, the whole of pop art.

Ewan MacColl in *Vox Pop*, B.B.C. Home Service,
20 June, 1967.

If there is indeed such a thing as an adolescent culture, its basic power derives from its capacity to counteract the adult Super Ego.

Jules Henry: *Culture against Man*.

Member of 'pop' group, overheard talking to his companions as he entered the senior common room of a Midlands university in order to perform for the staff dance: 'I'm not putting my gold suit on for this lot.'

1
Education and the Cultural Dilemma

The meaning of 'culture'

The word 'culture' is normally used in two broad senses. It is used by anthropologists to refer to the total pattern of a society's life. The ways in which men co-operate or conflict, their social and political institutions, their taboos, rituals and ceremonies, their ways of bringing up the young, their shames and crimes, all are regarded as equally manifestations of the culture, trivial or profound. Used in this way, the word has no implications of value—everything reveals the culture, not just a few selected important details. The other typical use of the word 'culture', however, involves a high degree of selectivity. It refers to a particular set of skills, ways of understanding, modes of feeling and to the productions, scientific, artistic and practical which enshrine them. In this sense, a 'cultured' man is a comparatively rare bird, sophisticated, well read, knowledgeable. He pursues a way of life which is only possible to someone who has undergone a long period of education and who has become highly literate in the process. It is in this way that Matthew Arnold uses the word in his book, *Culture and Anarchy*; for there he defines culture as the 'best that has been thought and said', as something which leads us to our 'total perfection'.

In this book the word 'culture' is being used in a sense which lies between the two. I do not want to include everything in it because that would involve a number of trivialities; so it is applied selectively to important areas of human thought and action. But in itself it is not intended to imply anything about the value or quality of these activities and thoughts. In my meaning of the term, a folk song, a 'pop' song, and a Beethoven symphony are similarly representative of culture; for music plays an important role in human affairs and all three are equally examples of music. We might want to argue, further, that some are more valuable forms of music than others, but we cannot deny that all three provide us with examples of a culture in this sense. In the same way, cricket, the differential calculus, carpentry, photography, the dance or crime would also provide us with examples of culture used in this neutral way. To speak of 'a culture', then, in this usage, will be simply to refer to a number of important forms of human thought and behaviour without any distinction of value as between one manifestation and another, and to the pattern of their interrelationship. (This notion of interrelationship is important, too, for changes in one aspect of the culture—the development of scientific thinking, for instance—affects the rest.)

There is a further point about culture that needs stressing. Our culture, for good or ill, exercises a profound influence over us. It organises the way in which we learn to see the world in these important areas of our understanding. For instance, it provides us with a language which in itself helps to structure our attitude to the world. And the various forms of our culture provide us with pictures of ourselves, our society and the world of nature, in ways which we assimilate as we grow up. It should be obvious that a medieval man saw the world of natural phenomena in a way very different from that seen by modern man. Thunder once

2

betokened the wrath of gods—it is now understood to be the product of a combination of purely natural events, and most of the terror it could inspire has vanished. When we think of different attitudes and feelings in this way, we see how important our culture is in providing us with explanations of the world we live in, and how it directs our attitudes and feelings as well as our ideas. Of course, we all add an individual and unique element to that understanding; but we are still very much at the mercy of what our culture *teaches* us about life.

Two cultures

Now, until the coming of industrialisation in this country, in the later eighteenth and nineteenth centuries, it has been possible to distinguish two broad cultures, using the word in the sense defined. There has been the culture of the upper classes based particularly on their ability to read and write. And there has been the culture of the ordinary people or 'folk', based largely on their traditions of oral communication. It is a pity that 'folk culture' even today, is still likely to summon up pictures of earnest middle-aged men and women performing staid versions of folk songs or Morris dances with breathy insistence; for of course the culture of the folk in times past had great strength and artistic merit.[1] It sustained a way of life which enabled people to come to terms with the rigours of their environment and the harshness of their economic position with courage and even gaiety. Of course, the talents of the folk showed great variety because there was no educational system to produce social stratification in terms of ability, pulling the ablest working-class children out of their environment and distributing them among the managerial levels of business and the professions. It was only the most outstanding who

3

attracted the attention of patrons aristocratic or ecclesiastical; the rest expressed their abilities in the community of the folk, in the excellence of their craft work, song, dance, tale and creative assimilation of long-standing rural tradition. There is evidence to show that verbally many of them were more sophisticated than their urban counterparts today.[2] Westmorland yeomen, Miss Mildred Campbell tells us in her *English Yeoman under Elizabeth and the Early Stuarts*, when engaged in a dispute over their tenant rights, declared that their landlords intended 'to pull the skin over their ears and bray their bones in a mortar . . . and when our ancient liberties are gone theill puke and poole and peele us to the bare bone' This vigour of speech indicates a direct sensuous awareness and a keenness of observation which stood them in good stead in their contacts with the materials of their crafts and the fantasies they translated into folk tale and song. They handle their 'fictions' with a stark directness which penetrates to the fundamentals of experience and reveals its patterns and textures. What they lack in psychological complexity they compensate for in the clarity and steadfastness of their vision; and they made their own culture within the traditions they inherited. The handing on in the oral tradition permitted individual contribution and embellishment. The village virtuoso added to what he received.

We must be very careful not to sentimentalise this culture or make it out to be greater than it was; at the same time, in saying this we must be equally careful not to dismiss its very real strengths. No doubt what has lasted and come down to us is not wholly representative—the best tends to survive; but what does remain is sufficiently remarkable to make it dangerous to condescend to the past. The people were sustained in their identities by a symbolism which penetrated all aspects of their experience and which they

4

accepted as *truth*, that of the Christian religion.[3] This provided them with images and moral categories of great emotional power, in terms of which they could interpret their
lives; at the same time they could project their interpreta-
tions into sets of common symbols drawn from a common
faith, which achieved immediate communication with their
fellows. Religion, too, had its darker side in persecution and
superstition; but it gave purpose to life. The folk were not
original in the modern sense because the unchanging nature
of their social lives easily translated itself into traditional
patterns and well tried forms of communication; but they
achieved a directness and forthrightness of utterance which
compensated for the lack of novelty.

In thus praising the culture of the folk, I am constantly
aware of the tension which exists between the virtues of
'rootedness' and 'emancipation'. The positive side of folk
culture lay in its comparative stability; and from this
'rootedness' its moral strength was derived. Its fault lay in
the narrowness, intellectual and emotional, it imposed on
its superior inhabitants; such obscure Judes were often
denied the 'emancipation' literacy could provide, and thus
lacked fulfilment. To some extent the two cultures did
interpenetrate, for both were sustained by a common symbolism and a common set of assumptions. 'Fine art,' said
T. S. Eliot, 'is the refinement, not the antithesis, of popular
art.' And so in fact it has often proved. Shakespeare and his
predecessors of the Elizabethan stage transformed the
popular tradition of the morality play; Purcell used folk
music—in *King Arthur*, for instance; Scarlatti was much in-
fluenced by the flamenco. It was only in the eighteenth
century when the Christian tradition was already under
rationalist attack, that notions of 'politeness' and refinement gradually produced more rigid classifications, so that
even the language used in writings was scrutinised for

vulgarisms and indications of low origin. Of course, court and aristocratic circles often looked down on 'knaves that smelt of sweat'; and the higher classes were often unconscious of the particular forms of folk culture. Yet, paradoxically, the universal acceptance of class divisions made people perhaps less antagonistic to cultural levels different from their own, than they have since become. This is not to say that such different levels were not recognised; but they were not categorised as a hierarchy of 'brows'. This is possibly because they weren't felt as a threat to people with different cultural levels; nothing upsets people so easily today as attacks on their tastes.

Furthermore, it is important to realise that sophisticated or 'high' culture is utterly dependent on the general quality of popular culture; it cannot maintain itself successfully in isolation, for it depends on being nurtured by a lively and vital participation in less conscious cultural activities throughout the community; the greatness of Shakespeare was dependent on the vitality of the oral tradition which fed him and which was represented even in the verbal misunderstandings of a Dogberry. For cultural health in the community at large each element needs maintain its own cultural vitality in a manner proper to its interests and abilities, and in ways which need not necessarily depend on literacy. What is required is excellence at all levels, not an attempt to make all participate in the same culture. The development of scientific rationalism, accompanied by technical advance, undermined the comparative stability of these pre-industrial cultures. Once the emotional power of a common symbolism had been replaced by the sceptical analytic spirit of the freely ranging intellect, uninhibited by religious prohibition, bound to question more and more the assumptions on which the culture rested, a certain disintegration took place. Two signs of this were liberalism

6

and romanticism; both asserted the atomic individual, his rights and his aspirations, against the common heritage of former 'truth'. As Sir Isaiah Berlin has pointed out in a series of recent broadcasts (Some Sources of Romanticism, Oct.–Nov. 1967), with romanticism the virtues of individual 'sincerity' were asserted against the claims of general truth. What tends to matter today (we still live in a romantic era) is not whether what a person thinks is true, but whether he believes what he says 'sincerely'. It is as if in the absence of commonly accepted standards of rightness all that is left is the integrity of the individual : it is for him to make his own separate peace with the demands of the 'real' world— except in matters where scientific standards prevail. Here we can know—the rest is opinion.

Scientific and technical development went hand in hand and led to industrialisation. This, too, had its profound effects on the disintegration of the old 'common' culture (defined in terms of the two interpenetrating cultures analysed above); and as it deeply affected the whole social structure and particularly the part to be played by education, I must examine its effects more closely.

The effects of industrialisation

Any major shift in human technical arrangements will inevitably involve altered patterns of work and relationship which will affect the whole culture. Let us look at the question of work, for instance. Work under pre-industrial conditions was often hard and unremitting; but a good deal of it was much more varied in scope than it is today. The craftsman selected his material, which often in itself involved a high degree of skill patiently acquired, and undertook most of the processes of manufacture himself, with the aid of his journeymen and apprentices. He was often

7

able to plan his days to suit himself; and most important of all, because his tools were usually hand tools, he imposed his own human rhythm on the work. He saw and handled the finished product and was thus able to see the results of his labour, on which he had set his personal mark and for which he felt responsible. Whatever man has, he usually wants something else; and the idyllic nature of this picture must certainly not be overstressed—as I have indicated. There were discontents and quarrels, bad and drunken masters, Saint Monday and Saint Tuesday, when no work was done, a savage penal code, shocking ill-health; but there were opportunities too, such as George Sturt celebrates in his well-known book, *The Wheelwright's Shop*. The skilled workman knew by long practice, though he could not have articulated the distinction, 'the difference between ash that is "tough as whipcord", and ash that is "frow as a carrot", or "doaty", or "biscuity" '. There were the satisfactions 'which, of old, streamed into their muscles all day long from close contact with iron, timber, clay, wind and wave, horse-strength. It tingled up in the niceties of touch, sight, scent. The very ears unawares received it, as when the plane went singing over the wood, or the exact chisel went tapping in (under the mallet) to the hard ash with gentle sound.'

All this, of course, provided a type of *education*, one, perhaps, which produced unconscious harmonies through the strength of personal identity it produced rather than through conscious awareness. The young apprentices acquired not only skills but a pattern of life. But, as Sturt himself remarked, 'these intimacies are over'. The new ways have produced a higher material standard of living, better health, more leisure. But they have split the man between home and work, introduced the tyranny of the clock, profoundly altered the whole pattern of his relationships,

8

changed the rhythms of his life. In his excellent book, *The Making of the English Working Class*, E. P. Thompson has chronicled the change-over from a domestic to an industrial economy and analysed some of the qualitative effects this has had on the lives of working people. When all allowances have been made for a slightly increased standard of living and for the undoubtedly darker aspects of the older way of life in England, Mr. Thompson is forced to refer to the process of industrialisation as, initially at least, 'an experience of immiseration'. And it was above all the loss of work status that drives him to this conclusion – 'long hours of unsatisfying labour under severe discipline for alien purposes'. Relationships altered – the distance between master and man increased immeasurably. The worker became a commodity, to be costed like other raw materials; he became an instrument, in that he had to submit to the rhythm of the machine. The notion of mutual *obligation* died, to be replaced by bargaining as the unions gradually increased their power. The cash nexus was all important, and money gradually became the dominating factor in the relationship of employer and employee. The freer rhythms of work under domestic conditions were replaced by submission to the factory bell or whistle, clocking in and clocking out.

Most significant of all, as industrialisation proceeded, more and more people had less and less to learn in preparation for their working life.[4] Clearly, at certain levels, there was an expansion of technical knowledge required; but for the ordinary workman or operative the machine gradually replaced the skills he had formerly required, until, by the earlier twentieth century, with the implementation of mass production methods and the assembly line, many workmen simply filled in what the machines could not as yet achieve—to be superseded, in their turn, by the gradual development of automation. This role of the workman was

B

explicitly recognised in the system of factory organisation known as Taylorism—the attempt as a result of the ideas of Frederick W. Taylor and Frank Gilbreth to work out the 'one best way', by which was meant the most efficient behaviour of the operative to help boost production. This meant rationalising the workman's actions with the aid of time and motion studies, and the effect was to turn him as nearly as possible into an addendum to the machine. Of course, since then, industrial psychologists have come to appreciate the harm done to human beings in this attempt to mechanise them; job enlargement, social benefits and greater opportunities for social intercourse have been devices by which they have attempted to break down the basic monotony of the work demanded. But the fact remains that much of what is done in the modern factory involves skills that can be acquired in an hour or two, or at the most a few days. We are far here from the 'niceties of touch, sight, scent'.

And, of course, this has all had its effects on the culture of the folk. For much of folk culture arose out of work or the relationships that work fostered. There were songs that were sung to the loom, or that celebrated direct muscular effort, like the sea shanties. There was the qualitative attention to the actual materials used in following particular crafts, and the discipline of eye and hand that 'working' it involved—as George Sturt indicates. There were the rustic crafts of the domestic economy which could occupy spare hours and enriched the pattern of daily living. With the coming of industrialisation, the cultural activities of the folk suffered a diminution. Urbanisation in the hideous nineteenth-century style abstracted the 'hands' from rural patterns of life into conglomerations of back to back houses; their understanding of country crafts diminished though, as Professor Hoggart points out, vestiges of the old rural pattern of life could survive for a time under working-class urban conditions. Nevertheless, as D. H. Lawrence saw, the time was coming when even the country man was becoming 'a town bird at heart'.[5] The old rural culture was being eroded (industrial folk music shows a decline in quality), and was being replaced by a narrower life of political association in trade union. This may have helped to induce the sense of mutuality which apologists for the working classes are never tired of emphasising as the characteristic mark of working-class life in our own times; but the skills and the 'niceties' tended to disappear, to be replaced by working men's clubs, the benefit society and the self help and assistance of the down-trodden and the poor. Furthermore, the restricted demands made on the machine operative helped to produce an element of apathy which tended to make him less demanding culturally : more content with restricted satisfactions so as not to induce too great a tension between working and leisure life.[6] As we shall see, even his mythic consciousness became a prey to inflated trivialities. The culture of the folk could not in any case have survived the coming of the elementary school, for this represented an alien culture.

A cultural error

The process of industrialisation, as I have just indicated, involved considerable impoverishments in the texture of everyday existence for many people; but of course it has also opened doors into other possibilities—or at the least, has seemed to do so. Although it involved such a diminution of work possibilities for many, the social, economic and political changes engendered induced our society in the nineteenth century to undertake an experiment unique in the history of mankind—the setting up of a *system* of education intended to lead to universal literacy. Of course, all societies have had their ways of educating the young, often under informal conditions of family life; for it has always been necessary to induct children into the habits and customs of the tribe and to prepare them for adult occupations. But nothing quite so systematic directed to enabling the total population to enjoy the fruits of being able to read and write has ever been set up before. A variety of reasons were given for this move, which in this country was argued throughout the century until 1870. If men could read the truth and exercise the suffrage, they would become more rational and even more amenable. They must all learn to read in order that they could understand the Bible. If only they could understand the truths of political economy, they would gladly accept the inevitability of their economic position. It was necessary to educate our political masters—and so on. But undoubtedly one of the basic contributory factors was the coming of industrialisation and the need to have workmen who could read and calculate—if only to understand the instructions relating to the machines they were called on to operate. Furthermore, the conglomeration of people into urban communities necessitated a rapidity of communication that only literacy could allow for. It was true that literacy was rising during the nineteenth century—some authorities have calculated that as much as eighty per cent of the population could read by the year of the great Education Act of 1870, which set in motion the movement to compulsory schooling; though how well they could read is another matter.

And indeed, the qualitative issue raises a question of profound importance. For the nineteenth century, in thinking about universal education, made an error of calculation of profound significance—if the phrase 'error of calculation' doesn't make it appear too deliberate. In fact it was a

12

natural mistake to make, given current class divisions and the lack of intercommunication. They confused the culture of communication with the culture of literacy. Let me explain a little more fully.

Associated with the written and printed word there is a historical culture of great verbal, emotional and intellectual complexity, a culture which, in general, has been the prerogative of a minority of the highly educated and sophisticated classes. Of course, not everything that has been printed is of this calibre—the chapbooks of the eighteenth century provided a sort of popular literature, for instance, for that growing body within the folk who could at least read. And a pretty inferior type of popular literature of a sensational sort provided light reading for the sophisticated classes during the eighteenth century also. But, naturally, the school has always been committed to the notion of quality. So, with some concessions to the age of pupils, the culture the school was concerned about was, in general, Matthew Arnold's culture, that of the minority, 'the best that had been thought and said'. As Birchenough said in his *History of Elementary Education*, the factors determining the elementary school curriculum have recognised the need 'to discipline the mind or give it a little culture'; and the culture was seen exclusively from the point of view of the educated classes. So that, in literature, for instance, it was extracts from the 'standard authors' which were to be read or learnt by heart. Matthew Arnold, who was one of Her Majesty's Inspectors of Schools, wavered between recommending Mrs. Hemans or Scott and 'something better': 'Gray's Elegy and extracts from Shakespeare'; for poetry he considered to be 'formative'. There was no understanding or appreciation of the folk tradition until the *Suggestions* of 1905 advocated the use of folk songs for singing, and included a list of suggestions. Even then, Cecil Sharp had to protest against the inclusion of many that were not true folk songs; he had already embarked on his lifetime's occupation of collecting them, and was therefore able to suggest adequate criteria in terms of which true folk music could be distinguished from the rest.

In the development of the elementary school curriculum, then, the powers that were had no sociological understanding of the nature, background or traditions of the new compulsory denizens of the schools and hence imposed what was, to all intents and purposes an alien culture of bits and snippets on people to whom, in general, it simply didn't make sense. It was against this situation that D. H. Lawrence, who was a trained teacher and taught in all for about six years, protested so strongly, despite the newer notions of activity and self-expression which had begun to filter into the schools by this time: 'Is not radical *unlearnedness* just as true a form of self-expression and just as desirable a state, for many natures (even the bulk) as learnedness?' And in case Lawrence should be looked on as rather an extreme witness (however wrongly), George Bourne provides more evidence of the unsuitability of the education provided:

> Its defect was that it failed to initiate him into the inner significance of information in general, and failed wholly to start him on the path of learning. It was sterile of results. It opened to him no view, no vista; set up in his brain no stir of activity such as could continue after he had left school; and this for the reason that those simple items of knowledge which it conveyed to him were too scrappy and too few to begin running together into any understanding of the larger aspects of life.[7]

Perhaps Bourne is to some extent at fault to expect 'understanding' of a section of the community which traditionally, according to Lawrence, had 'lived almost entirely by

14

instinct'. This is a crucial issue we shall have to consider later. But for the moment the indictment stands, not only because of the unconnected nature of much of the knowledge that was handed out, so that it failed to link with anything in the child's background; but also because the whole exercise was conceived in terms alien to the historical consciousness of the people. Even today, depite the attempts at new methods of presentation and the greater social awareness of class differences, the full measure of the problem has not been adequately assessed. The syllabus for the less able child at secondary level still, by and large, constitutes a watered-down version of the same culture that is thought adequate for the brightest.[8]

Implications of literacy

The foundation stone of the culture of the school is the book. 'Get out your books', is the ritual that opens the majority of school lessons, still. Nothing that I say subsequently should in any way be taken as deprecatory of the book as an instrument of learning—in its right context. Yet it is astonishing how little understanding we have of what is implied by the reading of a book—a book, I mean, of some quality, not the ephemeral offerings of railway bookstalls. And by the 'reading of a book', I intend to refer to the psychological and social conditions that make it possible, irrespective of content. It is only when we stop to consider that the vast mass of humanity, throughout human history, has not been able to read, that we realise how unusual an accomplishment it is; and we may, therefore, be led to expect that it is an accomplishment of some complexity which is bound to have an effect on the consciousness of the people which sets so high a store on the ability to do so.

To begin with, a book is something that, usually, is read to oneself. Of course, it can be read aloud to a group; but this, today, is unusual—except, sometimes, in schools. As the object of private study, then, it creates social distances. Reading means abstracting oneself from the social group. and concentrating on the words on the page. These words, of course, are simply visual marks which demand a knowledgeable attention for interpretation. They are quite inanimate and need to be decoded in the inner mind. To obtain their full flavour, such as they might have had in speech, a complex process of translation needs to take place. Spoken words carry much more in the way of meaning than is apparent in the plain prose sense of the words used. The inflexions of the voice convey indications of attitude to the subject-matter and to the audience; they transmit the interest or boredom of the speaker; and even plain prose sense will vary with emphasis. Think of what a simple sentence like 'He wouldn't give him sixpence' could imply in accordance with which of the main words receives the most emphasis. An important element of speech, then, is a certain affective quality, a tone or a nuance which is implicit in the manner of speaking as well as in the words said; and these can be incredibly complicated and subtle. There is nothing of this emotional quality in a printed page, except such as the solitary reader can learn to interpret from the clues he is presented with and such as he can project into the inanimate and objective marks he sees in front of him. The book is indifferent and, in itself, uncommunicative. The marks must be interpreted in the inner ear, and scanned and re-read for their subtleties. They stimulate only the visual perception of the reader, not his hearing; they exist within a limited frame, whereas hearing involves total immersion—spoken words reverberate throughout the room and can be accepted communally.

It is important to realise the truth in Professor McLuhan's dictum that 'The medium is the message'. His point is that different media of communication involve one in quite different psychological states of being, make different demands on different senses and on their interrelationship. The book stimulates the inner man; and with the coming of a book culture, things begin to happen much more 'in the mind' than they did within an oral tradition. Books have contributed a great deal to that psychological inwardness which is so much the characteristic of modern educated man. They have contributed, too, to his social isolation and to the greater evenness of his emotional life. Of course, what matters, too, is precisely what is read, and how much. But the mere act of reading means cutting oneself off, temporarily, at least, from one's family and friends. The library and study are rooms apart; and the lack of social intercourse is symbolised by the silence that usually prevails.

At a time when, if the diagnosis given above of some of the consequences of industrialisation is correct, it would seem that, at work, their experience, because of mass methods of production, has become narrower than ever before, it looks as though giving people the ability to read must have opened up worlds of interest and understanding that had previously been quite closed to them. To some extent this is true, of course. Many working-class men in the nineteenth century, auto-didacts, saw in the ability to read the key to all knowledge and understanding, and these in turn the true basis of the political power which, increasingly throughout the century, working-class leaders sought. Sometimes they would go to extraordinary lengths to turn to good account the bare ability to read they had acquired in the dame school. Thomas Cooper of Gainsborough, later leader of the Leicester Chartists, usually rose by 4 a.m., winter and summer, read till work, at work (when he could) and again in the evening. His reading covered a very wide field in history, literature, metaphysics, and he also mastered Latin, Greek, some Hebrew, and committed whole plays of Shakespeare to memory. Such devotion (and Cooper was far from being the only example) makes one hesitant of criticising the diffusion of an ability which bestowed such benefits on people who had previously been deprived.

Yet we encounter, in the earlier years of the twentieth century, a remarkable statement made by one of the greatest imaginative minds of the age:

> *The great mass of humanity should never learn to read and write—never.*

Such an astonishing injunction strikes at the very heart of our whole democratic educational effort. Our attempt, arising out of the industrial and political needs of the nineteenth century, has been to emancipate the people, afford them opportunities of enlightenment, open doors for their understanding. How can these liberalising efforts be reconciled with the categorical negative which D. H. Lawrence throws in the teeth of our disinterested humanitarian impulses?[9]

The failure of popular education

Let me to begin with allay any suspicion that Lawrence's aim in saying what he did was political, that he wanted to do the workers out of their hard won emancipation, that he was 'fascist' in outlook. He was the son of a coal miner himself, brought up in the mining area of Eastwood, near Nottingham; and he is probably the only writer of outstanding genius the working classes have produced over the last

18

hundred years. Nor did he ever lose his affection for his people. In general, he loved best working people and aristocrats, for they shared a certain capacity for insouciance which he admired in contrast to the everlasting moralising and 'caring' of the middle classes. So his criticism of their new found education did not arise out of hatred or dislike of his own class. And it must be remembered that Lawrence himself was a trained teacher and had more than enough experience of the classroom for a man of his acuteness to gauge the worth of much of what was being given to them, the sense they made of it, and their response to it.

When we consider this remark of Lawrence's, we strike at the heart of a twentieth-century dilemma; and the dilemma relates to the terms in which *it is possible* for people of very different backgrounds and abilities *to impose order on the world*. What I mean is this. Traditionally, various elements in the community have made sense of the world in very different ways. The ablest, I suppose, have always, in historical times, tended to make their sense in terms of conscious understanding. Where practical matters have been concerned, they have proceeded empirically, solving their problems as they have gone along, building up a fair body of theory in the process. To cope with their moral dilemmas and their deepest hopes and fears about the world they inhabit, they have invented myths which have at once explained their feelings of bewilderment and provided models of behaviour with a pedagogic force for future generations. Their more intimate, sensuous appreciations of the world they have projected into a number of art forms employing a variety of media. With the further development of consciousness, the theoretical spirit has spread to all aspects of human behaviour, so that, in addition to action, they have created a world of speculation about action. They have speculated about their myths, about

19

their art, about their social and political behaviour, about even their past. Above all, in our own era, they have speculated about the natural world they inhabit. At least, so the tale has gone.

The tale I mean is the one told by, amongst others, the great nineteenth-century philosopher, Friedrich Nietzsche; my analysis, in general, follows what he has to say about the development of the Greek Spirit.[10] It may or may not tell us a great deal about the Greek; but it certainly tells us a great deal about Nietzsche and his view of the nineteenth-century dilemma. For, naturally, he projected back into Greek times the tensions he felt to be characteristic of his own era: and these, by implication, he interpreted in terms of the confrontation of the spirit of Dionysus (the god of wine and, therefore, of primitive instinct) by the great exemplar of theoretical man, Socrates. What Nietzsche implied by this confrontation was the conquest of instinctual, spontaneous life by science and knowledge and conscious intelligence. Translated into Lawrence's idiom, it involved the perversion of direct sensual awareness by mind-knowledge and 'ideas': 'Because, if you think of it, everything which is provoked or originated *by an idea* works automatically or mechanically' (*Fantasia of the Unconscious*). Men were becoming over self-conscious and hence too inhibited. For an idea is always an abstraction from the totality of presented reality, and so those who were absorbed by ideas lost something of the wholeness and flow of life. Lawrence spoke thus of his father's generation of coal miners. 'The people lived almost entirely by instinct; men of my father's age could not really read. And the pit did not mechanise men. On the contrary . . . my father loved the pit. He was hurt badly, more than once, but he would never stay away. He loved the contact, the intimacy, as men in the war loved the intense male comradeship of the dark

20

days . . . He was happy: or more than happy, he was fulfilled' ('Nottingham and the Mining Countryside').

This, then, is why basically Lawrence saw the school as a cultural monstrosity—at least for his own people. It stood for *understanding*. Of course, he saw that for some, mind-knowledge, ideas, were the breath of life. He saw that they had to live in *these* terms, to fulfil themselves: 'Mental consciousness is a purely individual affair. Some men are born to be highly and delicately conscious' (*Fantasia of the Unconscious*). But, for even the majority, 'much mental consciousness is simply a catastrophe, a blight'. He saw that such people imposed their order on the world in different terms from those implicit in school subjects. He saw that they needed the discipline of direct contact, like that of old-fashioned craftsmen, and of participation, like that of the old rituals. For such, 'knowledge *must* be symbolical, mythical, dynamic'.

Here, then, we come to the quick of the dilemma. Of course, given the conditions of the modern world, we cannot accept Lawrence's injunction that the majority of the people should be released from the need to learn to read and write or, to put it another way, denied access to the riches of a literate civilisation. Such denial would be at once impractical and unacceptable to our conventions of social justice. On practical grounds at least, we require the literacy of communication; the modern world could not function without it. But, given this as a primary datum, there is no shred of reason why we should not show willingness to learn from the insights of a mind that could penetrate so deeply into the fundamentals of our cultural dilemmas. There is one very pressing reason why we should, indeed. *If we are honest, we have to admit that a great deal of our popular education is an almost total failure.* We just do not know what to do with a considerable proportion of our school population—'do' in a sense which will make any real inroads into the very quick of their being so that it exercises a profound and developing effect on the rest of their lives, so that it penetrates to the heart of their experience. Of course, we can arouse temporary interest with some; of course, bits and pieces may catch on, strike an occasional echo, arouse an ephemeral enthusiasm. But there are many, many children to whom school, as it is at present organised, is to employ their own idiom, 'a dead loss'. And the proof of this statement lies in the nature of the culture they concern themselves with once they have left school.

New modes of communication

For the school has undertaken its redoubtable task at almost the very moment when alternative modes of communication are offering their seductions to a public which has been making very heavy weather of the culture of literacy. Of course, there have always been alternative cultural offerings to what the school had to give. There was the pub, and there was the music hall, for instance; Matthew Arnold had complained that the lower classes were 'thrown back upon themselves, upon their beer, their gin and their fun'. There was not much evidence that many of them had been 'humanised', to use his favourite word, by their experience in school—as Ursula, in Lawrence's novel *The Rainbow* discovers. It didn't even work as communication literacy—for what emerged as communication turned out to be the popular press of the twentieth century, and the exploitation of the new mass market by Lord Northcliffe and the *Daily Mail*. Of course, the tendencies which were implicit in the popular journalism of the *Mail* had appeared some considerable time before Northcliffe appeared on the scene. But he exploited those tendencies with a new cunning and insight into what the people wanted—the sensationalism, the circulation gimmicks, the new typography, the emphasis on what it paid to print—in a word, the new irresponsibility in terms of the education of the new democracy.[11]

Then, technical advance has added new dimensions to popular culture. The cinema, the radio, television, all involved quite different sorts of appeals to that of print, quite different sense dimensions.[12] The appearance of the electric media has transformed the world of the ordinary person to a degree that can, as yet, hardly be fully assessed. I shall try to analyse some of their implications in a later chapter. For the moment it suffices to point out that they have certainly provided an alternative culture to that of the school, a popular culture, though in a sense significantly different from that of folk culture. For the folk culture was a culture of the folk, in the sense that it was they who created it; they added at least significant improvisations to long-standing traditional forms and modes. But the new popular culture is a consumers culture, in the sense that, by and large, the public passively accept what is piped to them from central distributing agencies—Fleet Street, Hollywood, the BBC. What is new also is the sheer volume of processed and packaged experience which is disseminated through these means, the incredible bulk of entertainment and information to which modern man is subjected. What is relevant, too, is the morality implicit in these offerings, and its impersonal nature. There is no question of direct contact here.

This, then, is the fundamental educational dilemma of the twentieth century. A traditional curriculum of academic and practical subjects, in general geared to the culture of the highly literate and sophisticated, offers its opportunities for promoting understanding to an audience of young people most of whose parents and homes assimilate a quite different sort of culture. The school has a difficult enough task in view of the complexity of its offerings; the extra-mural competition turns it into a well-nigh impossible task with many of its inhabitants. To this dilemma, then, we must address ourselves.

2

The culture of the schools

The discipline of the school

I want now to examine the culture of the school and that of today's popular culture in much greater detail, so as to bring out more concretely the nature of the dilemma posed at the end of the last chapter.

The school is heir to a very long-standing tradition, implicit in the whole Christian heritage, which sees in man an antagonism of forces. It is, of course, inevitably a moral agency; the notion of education, as Professor Peters has recently pointed out, has a value assumption built into it. And the morality it has inherited, both implicitly and explicitly, is essentially one of conflict. Accordingly, the child is thought of—or was thought of until recently—as being a bundle of urges and impulses, many, if not most, of an undesirable nature. Therefore he must be submitted to a regimen of discipline, so that he can be helped to control the more destructive part of his nature and give rein to the better, more constructive side. Various ways of expressing this would be to say that he must overcome the burden of original sin by which he is by nature oppressed; that he must conquer impulse and passion by reason; or that he must keep the Id under restraint through proper Ego control,

C

aided by the Super-ego. The aim, fundamentally, has been to produce a moral, rational being, capable of self-direction and self-responsibility, latterly to take his place as a free citizen in a free society. This picture of the child as a conflict of forces has been modified but not finally repudiated by 'progressive' ideas in education; but of this I shall say more later.

It is clear, for instance, that the gains of the school are long term. Before even their more tangible results—in the guise of examinations and certificates—become apparent, a good deal of disciplined work has to be undertaken. The pupil has to subordinate immediate satisfactions—playing out, hobbies, and so on—to later benefits. The work itself often conveys no immediate enlightenment in compensation, and it is not always as well adjusted to the psychological development of the pupil as it ought to be; it makes demands, that is to say, that the pupil can only imperfectly accommodate. It runs contrary to the interests and expectations of many homes and, at best, is supported there as an element whose function it is to procure future pecuniary benefits in terms of better jobs and the like.

All this—quite apart from other distractions briefly alluded to in the last chapter—implies a very serious inroad on 'natural' inclinations and propensities. Here lies at least part of the explanation for the fact that the classroom is nearly always a scene of some tension and conflict; and why concepts like 'discipline', 'rewards', 'punishments' make their way into the traditional pathways of the school. Of course, it is quite true that in fairly recent years, in the state system at any rate, attempts in some sectors of schooling have been made to work in terms of a rather different set of assumptions, in line with a rather different ethic. Here the key lies, not in the imposition of restraints, but in their

26

lifting. This stems from a different tradition of human assessment—one which asserted the 'natural goodness' of men and blamed their shortcomings, which are all too observable, on to the corruptions of the society into which they are born (how men ever become corrupt originally, if they were born good, was never satisfactorily explained). This line of educational thinking, which stems from Rousseau via Pestalozzi and Froebel, implied that natural impulse was a good thing, and urged a much less authoritarian role for the teacher: he should, according to Froebel, be 'passive and protective, not active and interfering'. He was to *follow* the child's spontaneous interests, teach through situations rather than by instruction, use the discipline of things rather than that of people. In this way one would inevitably fall into line with children's psychological development, and would thus match the logic of material with the growth of mind and body. It is an attractive theory, but, of course, it does not entirely work. Sin gets in somehow and the projected harmony of inner being and outer world breaks down. Authority is still needed, as even the most cursory study of Rousseau's *Emile* indicates; but the authority tends to be one of manipulation rather than that of direct intervention. It is still the teacher who must prepare situations—and, moreover, the *right* situations in the correct order. It becomes clear that it is only certain impulses that can be encouraged; it is still 'moral' rather than 'natural' man that we are concerned about. Learning of this intellectual complexity cannot be made entirely attractive—there is inevitably an element which may well be regarded as drudgery involved.[1]

The purpose of all this discipline, as I indicated in the last chapter, is very much to induce *understanding*. There are obvious exceptions to this. Physical education, various arts and crafts, a variety of practical skills (domestic science

27

and the like) emphasise doing rather than pure cognition; though, even here, of course, there is usually an intellectual, theoretical element. But the central core of the school curriculum emphasises learning of an intellectual sort—properly conceived, that is, because it often degenerates into memory work. English, a modern language, history, geography, social studies, technical subjects, mathematics, the sciences—these are the disciplines that play a major role in our schools. In their full development, they constitute the modern guise of 'high' or 'minority' culture. For less able children they appear in watered-down versions; attempts are made to integrate them in projects, so as to give a real-life orientation and appeal. They are displayed in their practical applications—French, for instance, appears as spoken rather than literary French. But the core remains scientific, technical, social and humanistic. The aim implicit in the curriculum, or explicit in government reports of the last hundred years, is to help children to learn to *think*. The emphasis is pervasively on cognition—certainly rather than on affectivity. It is, indeed, explicitly the aim of the comprehensive school, towards which we are inevitably moved by government intention, to provide a common core curriculum of mainly intellectual work for at least the first two or three years of the secondary stage; and, with minor modifications, this common element is provided for all children except the badly retarded who require remedial help. Again, treatment may differ from level to level, approach may alter, range and depth of study within the framework may vary; but, in all cases, what is done shares one broad characteristic—*it nowhere seriously touches those cultural experiences in terms of which a considerable majority are going to spend the rest of their lives.* Even the arts which are practised have practically no roots in the community at large and, therefore, exist largely as hothouse exercises. Where will school leavers find the opportunities to pursue any interest they may have found in *practising* modern educational dance, pottery, drama, even art and music? There are adult education classes—but these attract only a tiny percentage, mostly drawn from the middle classes. There are local art, orchestral and drama societies—the latter usually for ephemeral West End successes rather than for serious drama. Even these, moreover, are usually middle-class preserves; they are in no way integral to the cultural life of the community, but represent groups (often cliques, with its slightly pejorative implication) of interested parties who meet as strangers, sharing little common life experience except where their mutual hobbies are concerned. I do not want to deprecate the devoted efforts of extra-mural lecturers, society secretaries, producers and similar workers. But the totality of their efforts is still marginal to a central and healthy cultural tradition. The bulk of the population find their interests in football matches, bingo, the milder forms of gambling, like football pools, and the communications of mass media. Whatever is done in school in the name of 'creativity'— and all honour to what *is* done—has no real roots in the life of the community, and tends to wither in the out-of-school environment. The mass media comprise the real cultural life (apart from 'hobbies') of most members of the community; and they play little part—except as peripheral 'aids' to conventional subjects—in the cultural life of the school. Folk music clubs alone offer wider possibilities.

But there are a number of children who go to schools who are nevertheless perfectly capable of making sense of the culture of the school, and who are going to make some use of what they learn afterwards. It is unfortunately true, however, that they are not always given the opportunity for understanding, making sense, in any real way. The

subjects are treated, not as means to a complex understanding of our common life, but as means to getting through
examinations. The tutelary deity of our schools for the
more intelligent (both Alpha and Omega) is called G.C.E.
Examinations play an inescapable role: structuring the culture of the school.

The role of examinations

The modern examination is a crucial feature of our schools,
one which owes its preponderance to the needs of the
industrial–bureaucratic state.[2] Of course, long before industrialisation, there were means by which young initiates
were tested as regards their competence and the degree to
which they had acquired relevant skills. But the real proliferation of the examination system follows the gradual
democratisation and the opening of careers to talents which
accompanied the developing political emancipation of the
nineteenth century; and this, in turn, was stimulated by the
rapidly growing needs of a system of governmental and
industrial organisation which required a large variety of
expertise for its implementation. Examinations of the
modern variety really date from the throwing open of posi-
tions in the civil service to competition in the mid-nineteenth century; and, whatever criticisms may be made of
examinations today, it is important to realise that this con-
stituted a considerable victory for talent over hereditary
claim. Here was the ladder of opportunity growing to be a
reality; here are the first developments of that victory of
meritocracy over aristocracy which in its developed form
exercises us today. Examinations, indeed, initially, were
instruments of liberation; they have only come to seem like
bonds and fetters because their virtues have come to be
taken so much for granted.

They have come to seem restrictive rather than releasing for several reasons. As instruments of social mobility, means through which the school has come to take on its major role in the distribution of life chances, they have come to exercise a disproportionate amount of educational attention. Pupils want to pass; teachers measure their 'success' in terms of the number of passes their pupils attain. Whatever the idealists may say about learning for learning's sake, understanding and the production of the 'thinking being', the schools have very largely substituted their own realistic goal of learning for the examination's sake, and success gained in terms of the number of 'A' and 'O' levels. A recent survey in a South of England Grammar School[3] indicated to how little an extent the staff had succeeded in conveying their own values and ideals to their pupils; 'disinterested learning' is still what the grammar school, in general, considers itself as pursuing—at least, this tends to be the stated opinion of the staff, however little some of them may be concerned with anything other than the examinations. Their pupils apparently don't even pay lip service to the wider purpose; they know the rat race is on and they act accordingly.

This would be all right if examinations really tested what was important in the various subject fields studied; in the opinion of many competent judges, this is just what they don't do. Their conventions mean that there is an undue emphasis on memory and journalistic fluency; and the Nuffield investigations reveal that the papers don't really test the real benefits that the varied subjects are supposed to convey. A recent investigation by Professor J. F. Kerr, with the support of the Gulbenkian Foundation, into *Practical Work in School Science* revealed that, in the examining of practical work the tests 'encouraged undue attention to training in techniques, measuring things and getting the "right" answer . . . To some extent the kind of practical examination set was chosen for organisational rather than educational reasons'.[4] The setting up of the C.S.E. examination and current efforts at curriculum reform have encouraged a good deal of investigation into current methods of assessing pupils through the various examination systems, and have revealed many weaknesses, much dissatisfaction with examination condition, uncertainties in marking and rejection of the values implicit in the papers in the various subjects.

There are two further objections on rather more fundamental, ideological grounds. Some forms of testing have been criticised on the grounds that they tend to favour children from middle-class background. Such children acquire a fuller and better vocabulary and are thus more able to cope with verbal intelligence tests, which have in the past played a considerable part in the eleven-plus selection examination, for instance. The answer here, I would have thought, is fairly clear. The school cannot revolutionise society (*pace* John Dewey) and must make the most of what is offered it. If some children come to school better equipped verbally than some others, I cannot think that this provides an excuse for holding them back in the often rather doubtful hope that these others will catch up. Vocabulary is clearly fundamental to progress in school subjects—without the ability to handle the relevant concepts, children are quite unable to acquire the various disciplines, whatever might be posited about their innate 'natural' abilities. The fact that there is thought to be a certain amount of 'wastage' does not provide an excuse for creating further wastage. It is possible to direct other criticisms against intelligence tests, but this is not altogether a reasonable one. As verbal ability is so strong a factor in scholastic success, any clue as to children's abilities to handle language should provide a useful guide as to future attainment. The objection is based on social and political rather than educational grounds.

The other objection is made on social grounds also. Examinations, it is argued, stress competition rather than co-operation; they foster the good of the individual participant rather than that of the group, 'good' here implying the ability to get ahead. This criticism rests on the ethical proposition that what we want is a less competitive, more co-operative form of society. This proposition, like most such, is of so vague a nature that it is really not possible to pronounce one way or another. What we need to define much more closely is what it is we are supposed to co-operate about; there are certainly some things that we ought not to be co-operative about, as the Nazi régime would clearly and instantly illustrate. I am reminded of T. S. Eliot's dictum: 'Fortunate the man who, at the right moment meets the right friend; fortunate also the man who at the right moment meets the right enemy'. (*Notes towards the Definition of Culture*). Of course, it is arguable that this is a vague pronouncement like the other, that we need to define these 'right moments'. This is true; what is important in the remark is the realisation that conflict can be as 'creative' as co-operation. Education is not politics; in politics a major aim lies in the elimination of conflict lest such antagonisms should come to take on a more dangerous and disruptive appearance leading to armed force and the break-down of civil (and civilised) life that implies. But in education, the rubbing of one mind against another contains important cultural possibilities. The non-streamed class, for instance, is another political rather than educational desideratum. Bright children benefit from contact with minds of equal intensity. There are other ways of meeting the specifically educational criticisms which, not unjustly, are directed against streaming than that of simply abandoning it *in toto*.

The main objections against examinations, then, are educational ones. Examinations undoubtedly provide incentives for pupils who, quite naturally, do not possess the foresight to see the more far-reaching benefits of the education they receive. On the other hand, they distort the nature of the subject matter and tend to substitute success in the examination for the clarification which the study of a subject should bring about. But they remain essential instruments of allocation in a society that requires so many gradations of expertise for its running. They are instruments of efficiency—and, in a society geared in large measure to efficiency, they are obviously here to stay. Any assessment of the nature of the culture of the school, then, must give them a central place in diagnosis. They form the nearest equivalent we have to the old initiation ceremonies of primitive tribes, the *rites de passage* which marked the difference between childhood and participation in the adult occupations of the tribe.

The great public examinations, of course, still only affect a minority of pupils—a rapidly extending one with the coming of C.S.E., but still less than half. These are the prime sources of social mobility; they attract the intense attention of their victims. But there is another feature of these examinations which warrants notice. In general, they are supposed to be the marks of a general level of education; though they are the gateways to the professions, what they test is a general, not a specific or vocational, competence. They are tickets of admission; they don't guarantee a particular seat. Thus many—though, usually, not all—of the subjects studied and examined are to become professionally irrelevant. This, again, militates against their being taken seriously as modes of clarification instead of as means

34

to advancement. This can occur even when the examination is a very advanced, university test, and when it is in a highly specialised field which one might have thought had already caught the interest of the student. I am reminded of the story of one of my university colleagues. One of his higher degree students wrote a thesis on some aspect of nineteenth-century literature. On being told of his successful completion of his course, the student exclaimed: 'Thank goodness, now I shall not have to read any more books.' How much more frequently must this happen at the lower levels when, once the examination is passed, the subject is put behind for ever. Over thirty years ago, in his book, *The Sociology of Teaching*, Willard Waller drew attention to the packaged intelligence the schools fostered, and its relevance to the market in an industrial society:

> . . . it seems very likely that the intelligence which the schools reward most highly is not of the highest type, that it is a matter of incomplete but docile assimilation and glib repetition rather than of fertile or rebellious creation. How many star students are grade-hunters and parrots rather than thinkers! For it is not only in the grades that teachers give good marks to good boys; the conformed intelligence sells everywhere for a higher price than the unconformed. The intelligence most useful in the schools is that which enables the students to recite well and to pass tests.

He was writing of the American school, of course; but his analysis is uncomfortably relevant to English schools—to the school as a social phenomenon, in fact. One must, however, tread warily here; the ability to learn accumulations of facts has its relevance in the mastery of a subject; to hear some progressive educationists talk, one would think that understanding arose quite independently of the facts relevant to the matter in hand. At the same time, one is forced to admit that accumulation of facts, in themselves, do not consitute an education.

Academic subjects

My assumption all along, of course, is that subjects matter for those who can cope with them. Underlying my comments has been a view of the possible nature and function of the conventional school subjects which I must now make more explicit. 'Subjects', today, in some circles, are rather at a discount—as can be gathered from that hoary old cliché which is trotted out with considerable frequency, especially by primary school teachers: 'I teach children, not subjects.' It is as well to realise that there is no such process as simply 'teaching children'; it is always necessary to teach them something. The verb 'teach' requires a direct as well as an indirect object. Once we are forced to ask 'What do you teach?' the answer will usually fall within one of the recognised subject areas, whether the teacher likes it or not. There are, obviously, ways of breaking down what are termed 'subject barriers' so that the interconnection between different subjects is seen; but as soon as one puts it this way, the basic necessity of recognising subjects as such is at once apparent; only in terms of defining vertically various areas of study does the horizontal arrangement of the cross-subject project make any sense; it relies, to become viable, on the mastery within various subject fields of certain elementary classifications and concepts, which then become employable within the new arrangement.

And, indeed, classification by 'subject' is not an arbitrary device imposed for the greater bewilderment of the young, an unnecessary perversity thought up by academics for the purpose of staking a claim to their own territorial rights, but simply, in the early stages at least, the most fruitful and convenient mode of organising knowledge so that it can be profitably studied and can lead on to new understanding. The world presents to us an undifferentiated mass of data which only the mind can organise into manageable proportions, through a series of models and conventions which make thinking possible, let alone fruitful. Subject areas are made up of these models and conventions: experts may argue as to which are precisely the *most* convenient and the *most* fertile; but, all are agreed that some such organisation is essential to allow experience to be handled intellectually at all.

And it is learning to think, or otherwise behave, within an important subject area that forms an essential element in any true education. Here I am implying a wide definition of subject area—using it to refer to conventional academic or practical or artistic subjects; hence my reference above to 'otherwise behave'. All that is learnt in school, at whatever level, implies discipline, ways of organising material, conventions of behaviour or activity. We only reduce the chaos of the world to some sort of order by learning relevant concepts and modes of organisation; otherwise we could never grasp the flux of experience.

Where the more conventional academic subjects are concerned—the ones that make up the bulk of the school timetable for practically all our children, at least for a considerable time during their school career—it is, of course, not the ability to parrot facts that constitutes the essentials of education, but the capacity to handle facts, to understand their interrelations, to see the interconnections between fact and theory, to distinguish between relevant and irrelevant argument, to handle the concepts relevant to the subject with confidence and to see how they fit into the structure of knowledge concerned, to come to an understanding of boundaries, to see the links with adjacent disciplines, and

37

CULTURE, INDUSTRIALISATION AND EDUCATION

so on. Application rather than accumulation is the key to modern attitudes to learning; hence the emphasis on problem solving rather than on the acquisition of facts. It is more the pity that conventional examinations do not necessarily examine those features of subjects which are within the grasp of children of the age concerned.

Very often we hear such academic knowledge being deprecated, not because it is beyond the wit of particular children (it often is) but because it is thought irrelevant to real life; there is sometimes talk of ivory towers and bookish lumber, of remote specialisms, of being 'out of touch'. 'Life is the trade I would teach him', said Rousseau of his pupil, Emile; and he referred slightingly to the fact that

> Everyone knows that the learned societies of Europe are mere schools of falsehood, and there are assuredly more mistaken notions in the Academy of Sciences than in a whole tribe of American Indians.

There is a sense in which he might have been right; for, of course, the Academy 'knew' so much more on which it could go wrong. Yet what are these academic subjects, properly conceived? They are means to an understanding, at a profound level, of aspects of our common life. What are the sciences but means to an understanding of the structure of the physical world? What is history but a means to an understanding of the past as a means of enriching the present, so that we can come to see something of the continuity of life and learn something from the experience of our ancestors? What are the arts but a means of expressing emotions common to mankind, in which we can share even if we have not the genius to create? What are the social sciences but a means to understanding the structure of society and the behaviour of its people? It is nonsense to

38

juxtapose 'life' and the 'academic', as if they were un-related. It is true that academic subjects are not always treated in this way, as means to understanding our world; but that is the fault of the way they are treated, it is not inherent in them.

The development of the expert

Yet there is a great deal to know within any particular discipline, art or subject field; and knowledge is expanding at an alarming rate. Our culture, in any case, is devoted to the idea of salvation through knowledge; by this I mean that there are none of those restrictions on the seeking for knowledge which have marked other societies, such as our own medieval one, for instance, when the Church forbade the pursuits of certain types of knowledge as being con-trary to the will of God. (The cutting up of human bodies was forbidden, for example, and this inhibited the advance of medical science a great deal.) Most societies, too, have placed their taboos on certain sorts of investigation. In our liberal, open society, nothing is forbidden; and, indeed, it is assumed that the more we know, the better we are likely to become. We speak of scientific 'advancement' or 'pro-gress', as if the quality of our life were bound up with the sheer quantity of our understanding.

However questionable the proposition is, the sheer bulk of the matter to be learned presents a formidable task to the educationist and to the pupil. Indeed, it inevitably involves some revision of what we can mean by 'an educated man'. Formerly, an educated man was someone who had achieved some competence in quite a range of fields. He was not an 'expert', but an all-round man, an 'amateur gentleman' who wore his learning easily, but without dilettantism. His informed comments were worth having on general matters of common interest—moral, social, political, artistic and literary. He was 'well read', versed in contemporary affairs; he was Dr Johnson's 'common reader'.

But such a range of knowledge and understanding is not possible under present-day conditions, or, if possible, would exist at far too superficial a level. We have moved out of the age of the gifted amateur into that of the professional expert; even matters of common opinion, concerned with intimate matters of social detail, turn out, under the researcher's relentless eye, not always to be as they would seem to the ordinary observer; though that is not to say that the researcher doesn't often get things wrong, too. Social science research is too much in its infancy always to provide really convincing answers to social problems; but the feeling that somewhere there may be an expert who 'knows' makes sophisticated people inhibited about expressing opinions.

The difficulty is that the expert spends so long on his particular expertise that he has little time for general education, except such as he can dimly remember from his school days. The result can be that the great expert in one field can be quite uncultivated in others. Good scientists are often naïve in their literary pronouncements, philistine in their tastes, unsophisticated as judges of people. Indeed, those who, in terms of ability, may be thought to belong to the minority culture of literacy, would seem to belong to the intelligentsia and, thus, to possess some general cultivation, at least in effort and spirit, often succumb surprisingly to many of the trivialities of the mass media. Thus Mr H. L. Wilensky in an article in *New Society* points out that 'Intellectuals are increasingly tempted to play to mass audiences and expose themselves to mass culture, and this has the effect of reducing their versatility of taste and opinion, their subtlety of expression and feeling'. Out of a

40

cross-section of 1,354 members of the community only 19 could be found who had made 'rather heroic efforts to cultivate the best in the media'—and most of these were university professors.[5] Mr Wilensky comes to the significant conclusion (to which I shall refer more fully later) that, as most of these 19 had inherited higher occupational status than their colleagues—their parents were often from the professional classes—'it may take rather close family supervision over more than a generation to inculcate a taste for high culture'.[6]

The culture of the teachers

All this has a bearing on a matter which is rarely touched upon, but which is obviously crucial to the culture of the school—the nature of the teachers' interests. Here there are no research findings to help diagnosis—an investigation would obviously be extremely ticklish; we have to rely on extended observation and extrapolations from students' attitudes during the higher education that is to prepare them for their jobs as teachers. If the teaching body is intended to represent the high culture it is paid, in general, to transmit, the indications are not very reassuring. Most teachers come from the upper working or lower middle classes; and, in a number of cases, must represent the first generation of their families to undertake any form of higher education—or even of grammar school education. Of course, this is no necessary indication of cultural impoverishment; but, for many, it is culturally, an unpropitious beginning. Observation—and some research—at training college and university indicates a great deal of cultural apathy, a lack of interest among many students in the things of the mind, a lack of discrimination in their presented work. They want a degree or certificate rather than the cultural experience that goes with it. As long ago as 1912 Sir Herbert Read wrote that

> It astonished me to find when I first entered the University of Leeds that the ambitions of ninety out of every hundred of my fellows were crude and calculating. They were interested in one thing only—in getting the best possible degree by the shortest possible method. Their career was plotted out and they were careful not to stray from their line which marked an easy path through the world of knowledge.[7]

There is a good deal of evidence to show that many students find in the university an 'alien' environment, not understanding the nature of the demands made on them, or the nature of the rewards to be gained.[8] The colleges of education find it difficult to get some of their students to do more than the minimum of intellectual work—and this, in the more permissive institutions, is not always very much anyway. Of course, there are exceptions, brilliant students who milk their institutions to the utmost. But the evidence of philistinism and apathy gathered by those who have taught and examined in higher education establishments over a number of years is too strong to be gainsaid. And this question of the culture of the teachers is crucial; no organisational changes will improve our education if the teachers are not able to provide classes with vital cultural experiences.

The culture of the school, then, is geared to the demands of high culture based on literacy but structured not primarily in accordance with the nature of the 'subjects' into which it is inevitably divided to make it manageable but for the purpose of passing examinations; the need to pass examinations fosters various aims and purposes to some degree incompatible with the real task of enlightening the student within the subject area concerned. Furthermore, the culture of the teachers is often not up to the demands made on them. Some have little interest in their 'subjects' beyond what they are expected to teach. They are highly conscientious in helping their students to pass examinations —but resistant to changes which would make the examination a better test of understanding and application. Many students and teachers, indeed, belong as much to the world of popular culture as they do to that of high.[9] But, you may ask, is this necessarily a bad thing in view of the fact that this is the culture of so many of their pupils?

The pool of ability

Finally, some, while agreeing with my analysis of the demands made by the school, would argue that recent social science research would point to many more children than at present appears capable of meeting such demands. Such arguments ignore two things: we cannot easily alter the home circumstances and emotional problems which cause many children to under-function. Furthermore we must accept that the environment itself contains profoundly *dis*educative forces which must work against what the school is trying to do. These must be faced if we are to increase the receptivity of our pupils. It is to a consideration of these forces, then, we must turn.

3

Some aspects of popular culture

The debate on our popular culture has quite a long history.[1] Raymond Williams, in *Culture and Society, 1780–1950*, has traced the progress of this debate and has identified two sources of its development: industrialisation, with its accompanying urbanisation and commercialism, and fears arising from the political emancipation of the people during the nineteenth century. Wordsworth had pointed out, in his Preface to the *Lyrical Ballads* (1800), how

> . . . a multitude of causes, unknown to former times, are now acting with a combined force to blunt the discriminating powers of the mind, and, unfitting it for all voluntary exertion, to reduce it to a state of almost savage torpor. The most effective of these causes are the great national events which are daily taking place, and the increasing accumulation of men in cities, where the uniformity of their occupations produces a craving for extraordinary incident, which the rapid communication of intelligence hourly gratifies. To this tendency of life and manners the literature and theatrical exhibitions of the country have conformed themselves. The invaluable works of our elder writers, I had almost said the works of Shakespeare and Milton, are driven into neglect by frantic novels, sickly and stupid German tragedies, and deluges of idle and extravagant stories in verse.

In 1834 Tom Moore spoke of the

> . . . lowering of standard that must necessarily arise from the extending of the circle of judges; from letting the mob in to vote, particularly at a period when the market is such an object to authors.

In 1869 came Matthew Arnold's *Culture and Anarchy* which remains a classic exposition of the conflict between what was found to be implicit in 'our modern world, of which the whole civilisation is, to a much greater degree than the civilisation of Greece and Rome, mechanical and external, and tends constantly to become more so', and the claims of culture, which 'place human perfection in an *internal* condition of the mind and spirit':

> If England were swallowed up by the sea tomorrow, which of the two, a hundred years hence, would most excite the love, interest, and admiration of mankind, would most, therefore, show the evidences of having possessed greatness—the England of the last twenty years, or the England of Elizabeth, of a time of splendid spiritual effort, but when our coal, and our industrial operations depending on coal, were very little developed? Well, then, what an unsound habit of mind it must be which makes us talk of things like coal or iron as constituting the greatness of England, and how salutary a friend is culture, bent on seeing things as they are, and thus dissipating delusions of this kind and fixing standards of perfection that are real.

Arnold's theme was taken up again in the 'thirties of the present century by Dr. F. R. Leavis in his 'Mass Civilisation and Minority Culture'. The greatest English literary critic of our times repeated Arnold's indictment and implemented it by specific references to aspects of 'mass-production and standardisation' which had aggravated the trend towards externality which the new machine civilisation had fostered.

Since these classic comments, evocative of a considerable debate stretching from about 1780 onwards, the analysis of mass culture has proceeded apace. For a long time the attack came from what have been referred to as the 'moralising literati', literary critics, who, practised in the arts of analysing and judging works of the imagination, have deplored the imaginative poverty and emotional debility implicit in our popular culture. Their attack has been based on an analysis of the content of popular culture and an extrapolation from that content to possible effects. Latterly, the social scientists have looked at the phenomenon of mass culture much more with the problems of communication in mind. They have asked the questions: 'What is being communicated to whom and by what means?'; and they have succeeded in showing that the whole process of cultural diffusion and involvement is a more complex one than appears at first sight, in ways which I shall examine later. (Educational sociologists as such have had little to say on the problem; they have been more concerned with problems of class and educational opportunity and their relevance for social and political justice than they have been in analysing *cultural* life-chances. When general sociologists pronounce on cultural matters, they normally reveal their inability to conceive adequately the conditions under which a healthy culture can grow and develop.)

But, first, I want to say more about the nature of popular culture and to examine the social, educational and technical conditions which encourage its proliferation. For, of course, it is a phenomenon which depends on at least three conditions, all interrelated: technical advance, political democracy and a system of universal education abstracted from the real cultural pressures affecting ordinary people.

46

I have spoken about the last of these in my first chapter; here, I will concentrate on the other two; for the particular nature of recent technical advances in communications has had a profound effect on the nature of our popular culture.

Technical advance in communications

Man, today, lives to an unprecedented extent in towns and cities; the reason why this is possible lies in the proliferation of means of communication of varying sorts which technical development has made possible. Pre-industrial man, as I have pointed out, lived typically in the country and his communications were confined to a narrow local area with the occasional visits the limited mobility of the times allowed. He was contained, therefore, very much within the confines of his five senses. But modern communications—telephone, wireless, television—have permitted vast extensions of man's sensuous equipment. It is not only that he can move from place to place with remarkable rapidity; his ability to see and to hear has undergone a fantastic extension. Information about distant happenings, fictional representations, can be brought to his town, to his door or into his living-room contemporaneously or nearly contemporaneously with their happening. His living-room, even his study, no longer necessarily contain; the outside world can impinge on them to an unprecedented extent. It is not surprising, in view of these extensions of consciousness, that Professor Marshall McLuhan should refer to the modern world as once more a village, though this time a 'global village'.[2]

The older villager's experience was what I will term primary; by this I mean that it was through his senses and the limited extensions to them that he could encompass

47

through his primitive tools—axe, adze and plough—he arrived at what understanding he could. This was supplemented by limited contact with church and manor; but the local community supplied the focal point of interest, as it did for the Bedouin Professor Lerner encountered in his investigations into the modernising of the Middle East.[3]

> I am interested in news about my household and my camel because these are my life and my link with this world.

And again:

> All I need to know is here in this tribe and that is enough. . . . My business is only what happens in the tribe. Do you expect me to worry my head over what is going on outside our camp? We have enough news and activity here and we don't like to mingle it with the outside.

Lerner notes the pride and self-sufficiency of the Bedouin; lack of contact does not bring envy of, or a sense of inferiority to, the outside world, but rather a contempt for city-dwellers and the soft living the city implies. The Bedouin's culture is that of the desert and camel lore (there are about 600 words in the Bedouin lexicon for the beast); he has a fantastic memory for genealogies and tribal story. And in these strictly limited ways, he makes great sense of his environment as it impinges directly upon him, as Professor Claude Levi-Strauss shows even the savage was capable of doing.[4] In such circumstances men make their own culture in the sense in which I have defined the word earlier in this book; for a folk culture is one which arises largely out of the face-to-face interests of the folk, and out of their primary experience.

The detribalisation which has followed as a result of

technical advance has brought with it a vast extension of consciousness and an awareness of an immensely more varied world. But it has brought understanding of that larger world, in considerable measure, in processed and packaged form. For usually there is an impersonal element involved in modern systems of communication which forms something of a barrier between men and their extended experience. This impersonal element may be necessary as a structuring device to impose some sort of order on the incoherence and sheer extent of this wider experience. But the fact remains that modern man, for all his extended awareness, takes on, in certain respects, the characteristics of a consumer rather than of a participant.

This happens partly because of the complexity of scale. Much modern popular culture is diffused by central agencies over considerable areas of the population. It is diffused, moreover, by technical means which are very costly. Those technical means themselves exercise a considerable degree of control over the nature of the message that is being diffused, form an essential element in the packaging that is being carried out. I have urged earlier the partial truth of McLuhan's aphorism: 'The medium is the message'; it is a technical extension of ear and eye—microphone and camera, for instance—that does the job, and then disseminates what it has already structured. Or it is a particular arrangement of type, so displayed as to catch attention by shock tactics of size and spacing rather than through the value and importance of its message, that involves the reader and batters his critical faculties into silence.

Behind the technical device, handling it, making choices with it, are, of course, a number of human beings. What they can see and report are, in turn, controlled to some extent by the technical means at their command. And they are controlled by the technical means, not only because of its very nature, but also because of its expensiveness and because of the financial interests, commercial and bureaucratic, its 'plant' represents. The 'producer' and his attendant technicians, are thus activated in part by their sensibilities; but their sensitivities are held in check by the commercial nature of their enterprise and by the lack of intimate rapport with their audience. They must create for their stereotype of the typical listener, for they need considerable numbers of them.

The effect which the interpolation of technical means between participant and experience has on the former has been analysed, in a comparatively simple situation, in Conrad's quasi-autobiographical study of seamanship, *The Mirror of the Sea*. There he shows how the relationship of man with ship, wind and sea is altered by the coming of steam. 'A ship,' he says—by which he means a sailing ship —'is a creature we have brought into the world, as it were on purpose to keep us up to the mark'; and he goes on to consider, out of his own experience as a master mariner, the subtleties of handling the old sailing ships demanded, in deference to the direct impact of wind and sea. In the modern ship, a third factor has interposed between the seaman and the elements—a new power which, in some degree, has inevitably altered the relationship between the two—'The machinery, the steel, the fire, the steam have stepped in between man and sea'. There is a new factor, which affords many new opportunities, greater safety, increased travelling range; but there are also skills that are lost, realities ignored, and human potentialities neglected.

All this is to make the trite but often neglected point that for all man's exensions of his capacity to come to terms with his environment, for all his technical advance, a certain price has to be paid, whatever the benefits. The interposing between man and his direct experience of devices for the dissemination of the environment may introduce subtle falsifications of that experience into his mind. What the eye directly sees, it has a fair chance of assessing as part of the immediate reality of the external world. What the extended eye, the camera, is allowed to record is very much bound up not with what is there but with what the cameraman and his attendant technicians want other people to see, and what the camera, as a technical device, can record. It can show us the dead body lying in the streets of Saigon; it cannot convey the odour of disintegration or the sheer weight of inertness, because it must transform the three-dimensional into the two. The result of the camera-man's effort will witness both to the limitations of his medium and to those of his sensibility, and, as important, to his assessment of what the market will stand. In sum, the danger is that the direct perception will be replaced by its 'image'. I will explain what I mean.

The role of the 'image'

Professor Daniel Boorstin has devoted a whole volume to the analysis of 'the image' and its place in contemporary culture.[5] His book, he says, 'is about our arts of self-deception, how we hide reality from ourselves'. And our problems, he diagnoses, 'arise less from our weaknesses than from our strengths. From our literacy and wealth and optimism and progress'. He points to the rising tide of ex-pectancy that our technical triumphs have induced in us, and he goes on to analyse at length the list of 'pseudo-events' we create in the attempt to live up to our expecta-tions. What he understands by the 'image' involves the inflation of commonplace people, commonplace happen-ings into 'events' which become newsworthy, and then can be sold to a sensation oriented public. An event now is a matter, not of its inherent importance, but of the relevant choice of adjective, or the particularity of a camera angle. Boorstin, amusingly, quotes the story of an admiring friend saying, 'My, that's a beautiful baby you have there!' and the mother's reply: 'Oh, that's nothing—you should see his photograph'—amusing, that is, until one thinks back to photographs of Mussolini taken from below to stress the hard outline of the face and the jutting jaw (the very 'image' of power and ruthlessness) and one remembers what that particular piece of pseudo-history led to.

It is my contention that image-making in this sense of the inflation of the trivial constitutes a crucial element in popular culture, and that the technical developments in communication which make this sort of falsification possible are all too frequently employed as devices for the *distortion* of reality rather than for its transmission. Of course the eye can be deceived; but it does not usually lie so avidly as does its extension, the camera—the more so because to the unsuspecting mind the photograph, in contrast, for instance, to the painting, seems to be the very organ of reality. Modern popular culture in its purest form is to my mind manifest in the advertisement, which involves the selection of words and images (photographs) for the sole purpose of salesmanship. All popular culture must sell, certainly, in terms of either finance or of TAM—ratings; and we can see something of its essence in the deliberately created dream world of the ad-man. Here is the pseudo-event in its purest form—the day that is actually *made* by Cadbury's Milk Tray, the personal catastrophe avoided by the use of Lifebouy, the linguistic perversion implied by 'the most civilised toilet tissue in the world'. Here, too, are those snatches of domestic existence which, against a cunningly contrived background of household well-being, spotless, affectionate and euphoric, create an atmosphere favourable to identification, soften up resistance by inviting participation: You, too, could be like this. The fairy-land of whiter than white is in the grocer's shop only just around the corner. A diamond is for *ever*. Immortality is for sale.

Traditionally the folk have often preferred the sensational, the exotic and the mysterious to the realistic, the rational and the analytic: 'When they will not give a doit to relieve a lame beggar, they will lay out ten to see a dead Indian,' complains Trinculo in *The Tempest*; and Autolycus knows his market for ballads 'in print', with their absurd stories of 'a usurer's wife . . . brought to bed of twenty money-bags at a burden'. 'Is it true, think you?' asks the beguiled Mopsa. 'Very true, and but a month old.' We have progressed beyond this, of course. We all *understand* the falsity of the ad-man. But, alas, we don't always *feel* it. The intellect and the emotions *can* work in harmony, for the connection between them is often closer than popular acceptance of their dichotomy would suspect; but the feelings can hanker after what the mind rejects. It is not that we believe rationally in the exaggerated claims that are made; it is rather that emotionally we hanker after some form of the absolute. The appeal, basically, is to our mythic consciousness—the more persuasively since the great communal myths of old have decayed and lost their power.

Now I must explain what I mean by a myth.[6] The origin of myth lies in man's ability to project many of his fears, hopes and dreads—responses to a mysterious and often hostile world—into narrative forms which externalise these emotions and which have both an explanatory and a pedagogic force. Men, in earlier societies, were not simply expected to remember and narrate mythical history; they were supposed to re-enact it, also. Originally, then, myth

53

implied truth; with the progress of rationalism, both among the Greeks and in our own Western civilisation, our myths have been undermined, and the word 'myth' has come to take on its modern meaning of unreality; to call something 'mythical' today is to condemn it as untrue.

Yet, understandably, the gap remains. Science can only explain so much and take us so far. Men have powerful feelings and responses which require an emotional rather than an abstractedly rational expression or reassurance—I stress the 'abstractedly rational' because, of course, myths themselves have a rational element: they 'make sense', they employ concepts and symbols, they possess internal coherence. They are themselves rational attempts of a sort to order and make sense of an inner chaos of doubts and dreads, hopes and aspirations. But they employ these concepts and symbols for their emotive power; in as far as it is legitimate to split the mind into its intellectual and its emotional functions (and it isn't very far), they appeal to the emotional side. The decay of the great mythologies (among which we must count the Christian) leaves a gap, an existential vacuum. It is for this reason that some modern thinkers, in their agony at the disappearance of this sort of 'meaning' from the world, have found life 'absurd', something which has degenerated into nihilism and meaninglessness. When Nietzsche proclaimed the death of God in the mid-nineteenth century, he ushered in a phase of human 'development' which is still with us.

But for those who are not capable of these metaphysical doubts and yearnings, the gap has been filled by more fragmentary offerings. Those who reject or ignore the great heroic figures of the gods culminating in the monotheistic God of the Hebrews and his Son must find other objects into which they can project their inner feelings. We have seen the political consequences of this diversion of human feelings in our own times in the rise of the dictators (Hitler, Mussolini and Stalin). Western democracy, suspecting the cult of the great man, has created a number of minor 'images' on which to place its 'tin wreath'. In this, the process is fundamentally the same as that of the ad-man: the inflation of the trivial into the significant, the exploitation of the personal and the familiar for purposes of reassurance and compensation, the release into vicarious experience, the titillations of the 'daring' and the 'sinful'. 'Everyone knows, of course,' says Professor Boorstin, 'that a star is not born, but made'; and he quotes Edgar Morin's analysis of the process, concluding, significantly, 'Apotheosis: the day when her fans tear her clothes; she is a star'.

In this sense, the art of the ad-man, creator of 'images', manipulator of the affective response, lies behind much of the popular culture of our times.[7] The great myths, after all, were founded on profound human truths; they expressed in symbolic form permanent human conflicts, brought order into many of man's ethical dilemmas. Our petty myths nowadays rest on nothing more substantial than dreams and fantasies, unanchored to any sort of reality other than the power aspirations of an ill-educated democracy used to seeing its material longings fulfilled with little effort from itself, and deprived of any genuine emotional pattern of happenings and events which will serve to bring home some of the deeper truths of mankind.

For, of course, the modern creator of our popular culture will both satisfy and create a need at the same time; he will both feed the starved emotions of a godless people and, through what he provides, create patterns of feeling in his public through the affective force of what he provides. He knows how, through the power of language or pictured image, of rhythmic and harmonic sequence, to awaken feelings which exist to be exploited, and which can be

55

tempted to accept the forms he offers them. The effect is that analogous to what D. H. Lawrence ascribes to our education (by which he implies our general upbringing):

> Our education from the start has *taught* us a certain range of emotions, what to feel and what not to feel, and how to feel the feelings we allow ourselves to feel.

Psychic mobility

Crucial in any understanding of our popular culture is a realisation of its exploitation of man's dream aspirations, its creation of expectations, the role identifications it offers; for our modern myths, cheap and tawdry though they are, preserve something of the pedagogic role of the old myths. This is most clearly marked in advertising, of course; 'Buy and you will be like us', these tinsel figures are intended to proclaim. But there are many romantic roles offered in cheap works of the imagination.

The Romantic movement—and our popular culture represents a form of decadent romanticism—sprang from a need, within the decaying moral and political order of the end of the eighteenth century, to seek a centre of self, a role identification, that would be proof against social change and disintegration. The crucial element in romanticism, indeed, lies in this almost religious search for a central core of identity, for a definition of self that could lead to self-acceptance when the social landmarks were disappearing. It remains essentially as it then appeared—a movement belonging to a mobile society, when self-identity can no longer be achieved easily in social terms, imposed by long traditional and religious habituation; it is not an accident that romanticism and industrialisation stem from the same era, for both imply increased social fluidity.

Now in a world of shifting boundaries, it is increasingly

the imaginative writers who seem to offer images for conduct—and who, by a further sophistication, come to see
that the situation some of their inferior brethren have
created contains its own dangers of excess. This is what, for
instance, Flaubert sees in *Madame Bovary*, and Conrad in
Lord Jim. Both writers acutely realised the dangers implicit
in the limitless dream element in a developing popular culture, the extent to which aspirations were being exploited
and, indeed, created by a culture which had no responsibility to anyone except, as it were, the shareholders. So
Conrad shows that Lord Jim lived 'in his mind the sea-life
of light literature. He saw himself saving people from sink-
ing ships, cutting away masts in a hurricane', etc.; and his
cheap dream life plays an integral role in his disaster. Flaubert showed how Madame Bovary's dreams misled and be-
trayed her.

This sort of role identification with the heroes of cheap
fiction constitutes one of the dangers of our popular culture, not least because of the sheer bulk of vicarious experience it offers people. It is little wonder that Marshall
McLuhan refers to the young as 'data processers' when one
considers how much fictional material is put before them
through the various media. The tendency to confuse 'role'
with 'image', to project oneself into the identifications
offered by popular culture was not part of the experience
of Mopsa and Dorcas, despite their love of marvels. Traditional societies do not have the 'mobile sensibilities' which
characterise modern post-industrial societies. The ability to
project oneself into a number of different life-styles is one
that only comes as a result of habituation to a variety of
possible images for conduct introduced by the various mass
media. As Professor Daniel Lerner points out in *The Passing
of Traditional Society*, a Turkish peasant, when he was
asked what he would do if he were to become President of

E   57

Turkey, finds the question strictly meaningless and perplexing; he cannot even imagine such a thing: 'My God! How can you ask such a thing? How can I . . . I cannot . . . president of Turkey . . . master of the whole world?' In the same way, many villagers when asked where they would like to live if not in their native villages, replied that they would rather die than live elsewhere; they couldn't grasp the idea of living anywhere else, any more than they could think of being someone else.

This element of 'psychic mobility', which is characteristic of modern man, offers increased opportunities for social empathy and understanding, but it clearly has its dangers when it creates Billy Liars or Walter Mittys. As with Morgan, it turns them into suitable cases for treatment. And one undeniable fact about popular culture is that it does offer a wide variety of images of unreality for identification. Even when all allowances have been made for possible failures in communication and transmission (and we shall need to emphasise later that content analysis is an insufficient guide to what is actually being received by the participant), it is difficult not to agree, in some measure at least, with W. J. Scott's indictment of popular culture, in his analysis of *Reading, Filming and Radio Tastes of High School Boys and Girls*:

An acceptance . . of a representation of human beings in action that is so patently false must tend to create some misunderstanding in the mind of the young reader of the nature and motives of human behaviour. Further it compels him to lead a dual existence, using a part of his energy in an excessive emotional participation in a life of fantasy at a time when he needs to understand and grapple with the real world. Granted that it is still necessary for him to withdraw sometimes from the real world into one of fantasy, it is of great importance that

58

the experience given in the fantasy should be of good quality, indirectly extending his understanding of reality.

The experience of the present writer as a child bears this out. My relations with my peers failed almost entirely to tally with that I had absorbed from my reading of inferior literature; boys, of course, just aren't as the author of the *Gem* and the *Magnet* depicted them, but I took it that it was I who was wrong, not the reading matter. Further education and good literature showed where the error lay, in the 'lying images of reality', to quote Olaf Stapledon's phrase, I had derived from my reading and accepted, on a necessarily limited experience, as conveying the truth of the matters that perplexed me. I cannot consider my experience unique. The more imaginative young person must, to some extent, be beguiled and misled by the fictional behaviour he reads about or views on TV, however much, rationally, he may 'know' its falsity; the more so when his world fails to provide any commonly accepted symbolism in terms of which ethical imperatives necessary for successful living can achieve some emotional potency, and in terms of which he can learn to structure his feelings and be helped towards an ability to make those renunciations and repudiations he will inevitably be called on to make if he is to grow as a person.

The question of standards

Here I may be accused of preaching; young people must be allowed to make up their own minds; they must be left free to decide. No man can legislate for another; the teacher must not be guilty of indoctrination—and so on. But let us be a little clearer about what is at stake in the pervasive influence of our popular culture. Implicitly it recommends an ethic—sometimes, indeed, this is explicit, but normally it works through the images for conduct it offers, unobtrusively, by a process of slow erosion rather than by direct assault. For direct assault, as we shall see, is foreign to the mid-century ethos.

In the first place it flatters; it teaches the common man to regard himself as the ultimate authority on all matters of taste and morality. Here we see the influence of that political democracy which I noted earlier as one of the three decisive factors in the evolution of modern popular culture. When Matthew Arnold, as one of Her Majesty's Inspectors of Schools, went to examine the Swiss educational system, he criticised some features of Swiss democracy: it was, he complained, 'socialistic, in the sense in which that word expresses a principle hostile to the interests of true society—*the elimination of superiorities*'. The notion of superiority has, in our own times, succumbed to the intellectual pressures of Freudian reductionism (so that 'superior' people are explained away in terms of childhood deficiencies because they fail to integrate with the group norms) and to the dislike of challenges from outside the self which partake of any tincture that can be classified as critical or authoritarian. De Toqueville, early critic and analyst of the democratic way of life, noted that, in democracies, 'Every one shuts himself up in his own breast, and affects from that point to judge the world'. Politically we have institutionalised the notion of one man, one vote and thus maintain the, perhaps necessary, fiction that all are equally equipped to exercise their franchise.

Educationally, we have to face the inescapable inequality of the children sitting before us, unequal in attainments and in motivation, facts which a mere glance at the exercise books forces on our attention, however much, ideologically, we may seek to deny the patent evidence. It is not simply a matter of one child's demonstrably *knowing* more than another. It is also that part of the inevitable result of the educative process is to produce inequalities of sensitivity, of understanding, of 'taste' and responsiveness. There are certain studies in which this is so undeniable that it has to be admitted; but, in questions of emotional response and sensitivity, it is easier to dismiss difference as a matter of subjective impression; one man's meat is another man's poison, taste, being relative, is not to be argued over. Now, it is true that in these areas standards cannot be established with the firmness and certainty that the rightness and wrongness of mathematical statement or scientific formulae can. At the same time, there are arguments which can be put forward to sustain aesthetic or moral discriminations: the proposition 'this is good' cannot be reduced simply to the psychological statement 'I like it', and there are, therefore, implicit in the statements of the former variety, criteria for discussion which establish such statements as objective rather than simply marks of subjective whim.

Once this is admitted, once it is granted that not only conduct but choice of imaginative experiences in fictional form can be subjected to analysis and can be *argued* about as better or worse, the autonomy of the common man necessarily suffers a diminution. He is not the sole arbiter in morals and taste—there are impersonal standards that can be appealed to, argued over in relation to the circumstances of the case; and the arguments pass beyond statements of subjective inclination—they make claims of an objective nature which need to be answered or accepted.[8] It is little wonder, then, that our society is in something of a mess over the notion of equality. In education we proclaim the need for equality of opportunity—but prevaricate over whether it implies the equality of all to become unequal or subjection of all to an equal regimen, an equal educational diet. This problem can be noted in the comprehensive school. Not only must all go to the same school; but according to the theory—and practice in many schools—all must be exposed to the same areas of subject matter irrespective of the ability of many children to cope. The concept of the 'common core' curriculum, in the first two or three years of the secondary school, denotes the imposition of an abstract educational provision, derived from social and political principles of little relevance to the situation, on the living reality of children with their immense range of interests and capacities, deficiencies and handicaps, all of which need careful consideration in order to serve their best interests.

The new ethic

I have followed up some of the further implications of our popular image of the common man and the consequences of our sentimental creed which treats him as an ultimate authority in areas of taste and morals because this seemed a suitable place in which to reveal some of the educational dilemmas our democratic way of life involves us in. It is, of course, perfectly possible to interpret the notion of equality in terms of a greater equalisation of life *chances* without the corollary that this implies an equalisation of life *styles*. We need to think of equality in terms of what happens at the starting post rather than of what occurs at the finishing tape. Nevertheless, the debate about equality is interesting in the sense in which the pervasive flattery of our popular culture is reinforced rather than corrected by certain implicit assumptions of our intellectuals and certain evasions of responsibility that follow. The life-style of even the educated today, especially of the young educated, is marked, as David Riesman has pointed out, by 'absence' rather than presence. Their very lack of 'style' or flamboyance is matched by that of mass media performers and reinforced by their phoney naturalness—the throw-away, 'yobo' behaviour of the Beatles in mass medium interviews, the deliberate cultivation of the boy-next-door image by stars like Tommy Steele. Today we tend to exploit absence of personality—'a front that looks like a back', is David Riesman's witty phrase—as the ultimate in 'personalities' at all levels.

It is not surprising, then, that I should indicate that popular culture works by erosion rather than by direct assault—yet work it does. The twentieth century has substituted manipulation for authoritarianism—but we still tend to end up doing as is suggested. After all, how can we resist the blandishments? 'Let's get acquainted' says the first page of the booklet accompanying the Necchi sewing machine, '99 New Ideas for Creative Sewing', and, after this folksy introduction, we are in the mood to follow the first 'instruction': 'Sit down at the machine and relax.' Could tone and mood be better adjusted to securing acquiescence —especially when one's eyes are being 'soothed' by those 'lovely non-glare colours' which we are invited to note in the next sentence?

The appeal of friendliness ('acquainted') is, in any case, irresistible in a society which, in David Riesman's phrase, is becoming 'other-directed' rather than 'inner-directed'. The latter represented something hard and discreet, dependent upon individual conscience and personal integrity; the former suggests something more deliquescent and chameleon-like, more ready to take on the protective colouring of its surrounding social grouping. We are always being told that we live in a changing society; and in the approved vocabulary of the new age we need to shed rigidities in favour of a new 'flexibility' so that we can meet the future

63

challenges, respond to the altered patterns, adapt to varying conditions. At the level of popular culture what at once
reflects and, at the same time, encourages these transmogri-
fications is the notion of fashion, which is another of the
basic concepts relevant to any analysis, however superficial,
of the 'pop' world. The implications of fashion stretch far
beyond the clothing the term is usually applied to; the
impermanence of most features of popular entertainments
is notorious. The fickleness of public adoration ensures a
meteoric rise—and nearly as rapid a decline for many a
'pop' idol. As a civilisation, we are oriented to the new, to
novelty and 'originality'.

What does persist, however, is the ethic which underlies
this restless search for newness. It is that of 'fun-morality'
and 'impulse release'.[9] Again, aspects of the new ethic
appear in their purest form at the prompting of the ad-
man: his aim is to encourage immediate buying—hence the
pervasive atmosphere of hurry ('post this coupon *today*')
which informs so many advertisements. The modern newly-
wed expects on the morrow of the honeymoon the household aids and comforts it took his parents years to save
for—and the hire purchase man is there to serve his
bidding, encourage his immediate hedonism. Saving is out
of fashion—and inflation provides a reasonable excuse for
immediate spending. And, of course, 'fun' is a persistent
ingredient in the TV advertisement—those smiling mums,
those hearty, impish dads, and the close-ups of little faces,
ecstatic at every crunchy, munchy mouthful.

For the essence of popular culture lies in its stimulation
of a consumer approach to life. Material goods, entertainment, distractions in a variety of media—all exist to feed
without making any demands on production. Furthermore,
they exist in a sort of unstructured profusion, without discrimination of taste or value, like a perpetual Woolworth's
64

Stores, all heaped with goods counter by counter. The implications of fun morality and impulse release have even invaded the schools—things must be made interesting, learning must become fun, work become play. But alas, the school, as I have made clear, must represent a different morality. To turn it, too, into a place where the consumer —the pupil—assumes the right to command distraction instead of the need to seek understanding is to turn the school into not-school, to pervert what is inevitably and unmistakably 'given' in school subjects. The world implicit in work of the school variety is the stubborn, irreducible real world; that contained in pop culture is one manufactured out of floating emotions and aspirations exploited by clever men who thus feed rather than check the dreams of unreality.

Two warnings

Before concluding this chapter I must enter two caveats. My warnings have been uttered as a result of a general analysis of the nature of popular culture, and have, I think, been true to its over-all nature and ethos. But they need to be supplemented by particular analyses in particular fields, a quite impossible task in a book of this size. It is clear that there is a good deal of variety of value as between different manifestations of the media; and these discriminations, can only be made as a result of a close look at each field. A start in this direction has been made in Hall and Whannel's *The Popular Arts*: and, though I disagree with a number of individual judgments, it is useful to have discriminations of this type made in a field which is often discussed only as a mass phenomenon. Such discrimination would, in any case, be an essential pre-requisite to work done in school.

My second warning relates to a matter I have already

touched on—the question of communication. If we grant that the *content* of much popular culture is as I have described it, what proof is there that this is what is understood by the receiver or that it has the effect which might be attributed to it?

The plain answer is that there is no *proof*; and communication research indicates that it is not always correct to extrapolate from content analysis to effect without appreciating that content may be misinterpreted by the receiving subject. As J. D. Halloran, Director of the Centre for Mass Communications at Leicester University, has said: 'There has been a movement away from the tendency to regard mass communication as a necessary and sufficient cause of audience effects, towards the view of the media as influences working amid other influences in a total situation;' and he points to the need for further research in the fields of perception, effect analysis, social interaction, etc.[10] While we may well be grateful to the social scientists for their warnings, it is absurd to pretend that sometimes, at least, communication does not take place as the producers intend: that, though the receiving mind may well make modifications in relation to predispositions and internal commitments, social pressures and the like, it is possible to get the 'message' without too much distortion: and that even when distortion occurs, it occurs in relation to the 'message'. We would have to posit a terrifying degree of privacy, of solipsism, if we could not assume that often communication does take place, especially in relation to transmissions which are specially tailored for simplicity and lack of confusing complexity; after all, most mass communications are disseminated with a pretty clear view of the limitations of the receivers in mind. But then it is urged that mass media communications at most reinforce pre-existing tendencies—they are not the *causes* of psycho-
66

logical inadequacies. I cannot see that this in any way ab-
solves their producers from responsibility: these 'tendencies'
exist in most people—tendencies to destructiveness and
hate or debilitating fantasy as compensation for inability to
cope. To *exploit* them is as irresponsible as to *cause* them
would be. We are all imperfect creatures; popular culture
works, by and large, by playing on our imperfections, our
fears and hurts.

Finally defenders of TV, for instance, often claim that
the medium can widen tastes, stimulate interests and
creative activities. As Mr. Halloran says 'The evidence
available does not support these claims'; and he points to
English and American research which indicates a stereo-
typing of interests. He concludes 'as long as immediate
returns in audience size dominate the picture and we
continue to provide a narrow diet for the younger generation, then we are preparing the ground for an even more
stereotyped viewing pattern in the future'.

It is interesting that in American sociological writings,
effects of mass communication are taken for granted—that
there are effects, at least. A typical analysis by David
Riesman, for instance, will draw attention to the conditioning of the 'home, the school and the media' as if the
last named was an irreducible, unquestionable element in
formative processes. Our greater reluctance here to admit
media pressures arises, I think, out of traditional high-
cultural dismissal of media potential, as something peripheral, non-serious, 'entertaining' and, therefore, to be
dismissed as an effective influence. Opinion makers in this
country perhaps still feel themselves sufficiently in touch
with serious cultural standards to enable them to by-pass
the growing pervasiveness of mass cultural modes. This is
both a strength and a weakness: a strength because people
have something with which to resist mass appeals, a

weakness because they fail to detect the pressure of events. The Americans, a more open society and longer habituated to the egalitarian process, have not been able to erect the same defences and therefore view the potential (and actuality) of the situation in a truer light. After all, outside the immediate groupings of family and friends the media are probably the most powerful influences affecting the lives of ordinary people today. It is clear, at least, that the school cannot compete in terms of genuine responsiveness and involvement.

This has not been an easy chapter to write. For, just as there are stereotypes of mass culture, so there are the stereotypes *about* mass culture; as Robert Warshow has said, 'As the mass audience escapes into easy sentiment, so the educated audience escapes into ideas'. And, in any case, we are so wrapped around by the presence of mass culture that it is difficult to free one's experience from the conditioning such culture provides: to the problems one normally finds in articulating one's reactions to what is part of one's growth and part of one's background, one adds the dangers of hypocrisy about rejecting what, in other contexts, one would quite naturally accept. There is no harm in entertainment as Shakespeare provided it. 'Fun' suggests a positive refreshment that no one can deny the need for; it is, sometimes, more blessed to release impulses than to restrain them in favour of a frozen conventionality which masks inhumanity in the guise of correctness. And there is nothing wrong in commercial transactions—we all need to live and there is no shame in being paid for our services. One can only urge that these notions and concepts of mass culture that I have analysed imply excesses that transcend their normal decorum; and that in such circumstances they become threats rather than fulfilments.

This is hardly surprising when our contact with the real

world in what is one of the fundamental human modes, that of work, has suffered so much of a diminution, as I indicated in Chapter I. In the factory, for instance, a lot of what is produced results not from a tool which a man controls and on which he imposes his own rhythm, thus making direct contact with the nature of materials, and using what becomes an extension of his human limb, but from a machine which imposes *its* rhythm on the human being, which demands only the limited attention and guidance implied in the phrase, machine-minder, and which handles materials in its own terms. In such circumstances, as Arthur Seaton discovered in Allan Sillitoe's *Saturday Night and Sunday Morning*: 'You went off into pipe-dreams for the rest of the day . . . You lived in a compatible world of pictures which passed through your mind like a magic-lantern . . . an amok that produced all sorts of agreeable visions.' This is not work that helps people to create a culture, except by indirect and impersonal means. The goods produced by machinery constitute part of a new culture, of course. But, even at best, they manifest standard-isation and uniformity, allowing of no personal quirk or quiddity, no individual 'happiness beyond the reach of art'. The individual workman, is not, except in the most minimal terms, involved in the process.

Here, then, is a situation which deprived the worker of certain sorts of satisfaction; and, at the same time, lays him open to particular sorts of cultural exploitation. The vacuum which much of modern work leaves in the minds of the operatives, both factory and clerical, creates a need as well as an opportunity. John Dewey, naïvely, thought that 'mechanically automatic operations in industry' might well free the mind 'for a higher order of thinking'. He failed in his assessment of what the mind, once freed from attention to the operations in hand, would do. It would not, in general, proceed to operate in logical thinking but in day-dreaming; and this for two reasons: because logical thinking demands an order of concentration and a skill in operation that most people demonstrably do not have, and because the interests of most people are affective rather than intellectual in nature. It is this openness to affectivity that must provide the clue to a solution to our educational problems.

Culture and the adolescent

But before we turn to this, one last point must be made. A good deal of pop culture is directed especially at the young. The notion of the 'teen-ager' as manifest in a special group with definable interests constitutes a comparatively new phenomenon in our society. He opens up a new market for exploitation. It is therefore hardly surprising that we can note the emergence of distinctive youth sub-cultures in the affluent societies of the West. As Mr J. S. Coleman has pointed out in *The Adolescent Society*: 'Adolescent social climates have their own norms and values—ones which may differ radically from those governing adult society.' The precise degree of definition which can be given to this sub-culture may be a matter for dispute; but it is hardly surprising that the immaturity of popular culture should make a rather special appeal to the young. There is therefore a very special sense in which the teacher is faced with the challenge of popular culture, as one peculiarly adapted in some ways, to the susceptibilities of his charges.

4

Conclusion

The appeal to the emotions

The culture of the people, then, is one which, generally speaking, appeals to the emotions. I have tried to show that, all too often, it is a cheap and tawdry culture, likely to betray one's sense of emotional reality, erecting 'images' of no substance between the individual and his attempts to grapple with the real world of relationships, inhibiting true empathy or fostering a debilitating sentimentality.

Yet this too has to be said. This culture is enormously appealing, in the emotionally undereducated environment we inhabit. It clearly 'gets' young people to an extent that school achieves but rarely—and that with an unusual child. 'It is *our* music', as a teen-ager said in a recent series of radio programmes on 'pop' music (*Vox Pop*, an extended investigation into the 'pop' world). And such music provides a focal point for teen-age rebelliousness, gives them a sense of warmth and togetherness, enables them to throw off the inhibitions of growing complexities and responsibilities. Such music of pop groups—compared to that say of the 'thirties—is insistent, compelling, mechanically dynamic and tribal—classless and faceless; and yet unlike genuine native music, it is unsubtle and unrewarding. It faces us with an immense task of emotional education—a task which the school, at present, largely shirks. For there is a sense in which 'pop' culture supplies a 'need'—for communal activity, for the release of energy, for emotional involvement. It is not these things but the *quality* of what is supplied that is in question.

An aim for education

The purposes of education can be stated in a number of ways, but one of the most important lies in the need to induct children into various of the areas of reality, social and physical, which, willy-nilly, they inhabit. Science takes care of physical reality. It produces models of the behaviour of matter which are as near to our understanding of the way the physical universe 'works' as we are capable of reaching. It depends on various sorts of measurement and it is abstract in the sense that it does not deal with the actual world in its qualitative fullness, but abstracts certain regularities of behaviour from the totality of presented phenomena for the purpose of measurement and categorisation. It is always basically hypothetical because refined observation or different modes of grouping the phenomena may produce different, more refined results. There is, therefore, a sense in which science is never quite 'true', but it is as true as our intelligence (and our instruments) can make it. We must be always ready to re-assess our findings, however, and to accept more refined models.

There is also an order, a 'truth' of the emotions possible—again never completed but always prepared for re-assessment in the light of a rarely perceptive individual or the changed emphasis of an age. And yet great art both folk and 'high' (I use the word in its general sense rather than with particular reference to painting) reveals, under the

72

superficial appearances of 'character' or 'tale', of 'mode' or 'style', permanent 'truths' about the human condition. Which is why when the foremost psychologist of the twentieth century thought he had discovered a crucial feature of human development he gave it a name drawn from Greek myth and drama—the Oedipus complex. After all, did he not say, at the celebration for his seventieth birthday: 'The poets and philosophers before me discovered the unconscious. What I discovered was the scientific method, by which the unconscious can be studied' (quoted in Trilling, *The Liberal Imagination*).

These arts work through a variety of media—words or pigment, musical notation or some material substance such as stone or wood. Yet they have this in common—that they strive, in their various media, to express intuitions about the world which are primarily emotional in origin. And when they are examined, responded to, inwardly received, they help to educate the emotions.

The education of the emotions

This is a phrase about which there are a number of very loose and woolly ideas.[1] For one thing, as I have hinted from time to time in the foregoing, these various ways of coming to terms with some of our deepest feelings about the world have a rational as well as an emotional component. They are not mindless outpourings through their media, but rely on such intellectual elements as pattern, planned repetition, form and order. If they are expressive of emotion, it is of an emotion 'recollected in tranquillity' —which implies an element of assimilation and assessment, of shaping and structuring once the original passion has quietened down. In the writing of a poem or the painting of a picture, there are conscious as well as unconscious

F

elements, conventions of statement which aid concentration and which need to be *known*. If there is a happiness beyond the reach of art, there is the conscious art in terms of which the inchoate emotions take on form and significance, refining themselves in the process of articulation. As Professor Edgar Wind says in his *Art and Anarchy*: 'Great artists have always been intellectually quick. The popular belief that musicians cannot think, or that painters have no verbal facility is a picturesque superstition completely disproved by the evidence of history, both past and present.' The notion of the vague, remote artist, mindless and untouched by mundane issues, is a romantic fabrication with little basis in experience: 'Precision is one of the ingredients of genius.'

When, then, we speak of 'educating the emotions', we do not imply that intellectual elements are unimportant. What matters is the sort of use to which these aspects of rationality are utilised. Emotions, after all, are directed towards objects or situations. It is rare that we are just afraid—we are afraid of spiders or the dark; we rarely just love—we love X or Y or even ourselves. And one elementary way in which we can educate our emotions is by altering our view of the object in a way which is partly intellectual. Thus we may love X until we come to assess her motives and her behaviour a little more deeply; and then we may find that she is just a little gold-digger and become disillusioned. Or we may hate coloured people until we realise that they are more like us than we had appreciated, and that they won't murder us in our beds if we let them into our houses.

But there is more to the education of the emotions than simply cognitive adjustment. Emotions, indeed, can be informative—our emotional reactions *can* tell us things about situations that our cooler reason might ignore; we

74

may distrust, be warned off an acquaintance by our feelings when all the rational elements in the situation point to the benefit to be derived from the relationship. Our feelings, attractions or repulsions, are often capable of articulation. They may be expressed very primitively in grunts or growls, coos or hurrahs; or they can be expressed in terms of some conventional symbolisations and rhythms, like much folk poetry. Or they can become manifest in more personally chosen symbols, images or metaphors and take on an individual rhythmical accent. In this manner they will make sense in a way which must in part, at least, invite cognition; they will say something, though say it in a way which is mainly controlled by emotion, not intellect.

Over the centuries, bodies of work involving different sorts of accepted symbolisation have been built up in myth, literature, and a variety of arts, such as painting, music, sculpture and dance. In each case the emotion is *articulated*, not allowed to evaporate into formless mouthings or gesticulations. In the process of articulation the original emotion can become—and usually does become—refined so that what results is expressive of emotion, rather than actual emotion. This is what Wordsworth implied when he spoke of 'emotion recollected in tranquillity', what Eliot meant when he spoke of poetry involving an escape from emotion. For it has to be remembered that though we categorise emotions under a variety of headings—fear, hate, love—not all fears are the same fear, nor all loves the same love. The exploration of the potential within an area covered by a general emotional term, such as 'fear', is what the 'artist' undertakes, so that we learn to distinguish between different manifestations of the 'same' fear of God (say): from the Biblical awe of

Batter my heart, three person'd God; for, you

> As yet but knock, breathe, shine and seek to mend;
> That I may rise, and stand, o'erthrow me, and bend
> Your force, to break, blow, burn and make me new.

to the gentle dread of

> Love bade me welcome; but my soul drew back,
> Guilty of dust and sin . . .

These are not literal statements about the world; no one could expect the deity, literally, to use any sort of physical force on his person; and it is difficult to know how one's *soul* could be *guilty* of dust. What happens is that the different emotions of fear (awe in the one case, a shy reticence in the other) are expressed through symbols which exist both for their sense and for the part they can play in the rhythmical pattern and sound which adds its 'meaning' to the sense. Language, in some of its uses, may be said to involve a refinement of primitive yells and cries, sighs and groans. Different uses of language at different levels of implication explore different sophistications of the 'same' emotion—or the emotion to which is attributed the same generic term. And what is true of language is true of a variety of other media. What we mean by 'refinement' needs to be argued in particular cases, for the word carries obvious value implications. But it should not be difficult to demonstrate that Donne's *Songs and Sonnets* represent a more 'refined' (more complex, more varied, 'truer' to the multi-faceted character of the emotion) version of the state of love than do the lyrics in any number of modern 'pop' songs.

In this sense, 'truth' is as relevant to our emotions as to our intellects. The articulations of great artists (folk and 'high') present us with feelings which we recognise, as we develop, to be true to our own deepest experience; and it is

76

a presentation, not a telling about, which they offer. Our acceptance, that is, is not simply cognitive; it is itself emotional, so that the artist seems to express what remains inchoate in our less precise consciousness. For, it must be insisted again 'precision is one of the ingredients of genius'. Human development proceeds, in part at least, out of an ability to make finer and finer discriminations. Even to primitive man, presumably, not all dreads were the same dread, nor all hopes the same hope; but he perhaps lacked the artistic sophistication necessary to define the distinctions possible among similarly named emotional states; through this later, more sophisticated sort of definition, an emotion becomes a much more precise emotion, distinguishable among the many sorts of precise feelings one could experience under the same generic term.

In this way, our emotions can be educated in two ways. We can become more aware of the feelings we have and we may also be able to develop new sorts of feeling. The literature, music and dance of the eighteenth century can articulate feelings for us that are rare in the modern world—feelings relevant to notions of grace, decorum, self-restraint, patterns of movement and sound that speak of gravity, dignity and self-confidence, very necessary antidotes in a world given over to heady restlessness and insecure self-indulgences.

Creativity: its implications

So affect is communicable; if only we can sufficiently employ—employ with deep appreciation and understanding, so that our emotion helps to open up the emotions of our charges—the right rhetorics, we may do a little to rescue our children from the sadly restricted possibilities implicit in their modern pop culture. As D. H. Lawrence appreciated, we learn to feel much of what we do feel through the persuasions and articulations of the rhetorics we encounter. The emotions of children can, within limits, be helped to feel what we want them to feel through processes of involvement and participation—I speak now, of course, of 'normal' children; the disturbed child needs the therapist, which is not the teacher's job. It should be as important to protect children from examples of cheap feeling as it is to keep them from examples of shoddy thinking. As Susanne Langer puts it in *Feeling and Form*:

> People who are so concerned for their children's scientific enlightenment that they keep Grimm out of the library and Santa Claus out of the chimney, allow the cheapest art, the worst of bad singing, the most revolting sentimental fiction to impinge on the children's minds all day and every day, from infancy. If the rank and file of youth grows up in emotional cowardice and confusion, sociologists look to economic conditions or family relations for the cause of this deplorable 'human weakness', but not to the ubiquitous influence of corrupt art, which steeps the average mind in a shallow sentimentalism that ruins what germs of true feeling might have developed in it.

Their education should be a matter of involvement in the forms invented and spelt out by others. But they must be given opportunities for the creative exploration of various media in their own right—poetry writing as well as reading, painting as well as looking at the works of others, music-making as well as listening, movement exploration as well as watching the patterns created by others.

This seems commonplace advice, for has not some of this become the practice of every infant school, sometimes even of the junior departments? Yet there is perhaps no concept in the educationist's vocabulary more sinned against

78

than creativity. Almost any nonsense the children undertake can be justified by such umbrella terms as 'discover-
ing', 'exploration' and the like. 'They wanted to make a
submarine', the teacher will say indulgently, indicating a
chaos of bricks and an apathy of constructional effort.
'*They*'re exploring materials', she will add, pointing to a
witches' brew of old cereal packets, matchboxes and Gloy.
Both 'exploration' and 'making' involve a framework—of
human effort and of structural implication. Yet, all too
often, what these children are doing is threshing round in
a void, unhindered and unhelped by anyone who really
knows about the constructional possibilities of bricks and
other materials. True 'exploration' implies a conceptual
framework which will at least begin to make sense of what
is being investigated.

This, of course, is not a plea for the too early introduction of technique; but 'creativity' in any true sense of the
word implies both limitation and precision, words which
seem at odds with its normal implications of fecundity
and expansiveness. Perhaps the best way of describing what
is wanted is to appeal to the need for structure. Even if
children are 'exploring', 'finding out for themselves', the
materials involved must be presented in such a way that
genuine discovery is possible, not simply a haphazard
manipulation which is ultimately boring and frustrating.
The children need to be fed with ideas and possibilities—or
to have them drawn out by questioning and encourage-
ment. Once the school was all limitation and instruction—
it should not go to the opposite extreme of formlessness and
disruption. An old packet of 'Kellog's Corn Flakes' has considerable potential, but not unlimited ones; the very limits
need to be utilised as creative elements spurring on a more
precise understanding and utilisation. We don't want to
extend the 2–3-year-old's need simply to mess about into the

79

school years—which is what happens all too often. We must not accept the assumption, too frequently made, that *everything* a child does in the infant school is somehow creatively significant; a child can 'express' triviality and apathy as much as anything else, unless he learns to follow orderly pathways; it is the job of the school to help him to find that order, which is, paradoxically, not a repressive but a creative thing.

For this developing precision in creative work forms a crucial element in the education of the emotions; creative work is a means of *defining* emotional possibilities; and whereas we cannot go on functioning all the time at the highest creative levels, such levels do provide touchstones of orderliness and resolution of feeling in terms by which to judge our more everyday feelings. 'Love' is many things, as the great poets make us feel: it is rarely the indiscriminateness of feeling associated with the 'moon-june' (or 'you-blue') syndrome of popular song. To have realised the former as part of the real truth of one's own life is to do a little, at least, to guard against the dangers of the latter.

So let us urge the right sort of 'creativity'—and in a variety of modes. Words, of course, are not the only medium; some children can express themselves better in other media: all need to try other ways: music, clay, materials, paint and so on. Even—I had almost said 'especially'—through bodily movement. The offence of the miniskirt is not its sexual provocativeness—women will always find a way to provoke and an ankle can be as disturbing as a thigh—but its gracelessness. Man reduced to the level of 'poor bare forked animal' lacks the richness that only the forms of human culture can give; and some of the forms spring out of the wearing of clothes and the discipline some clothes, at least, provide. Movement, furthermore, has wider creative possibilities—as the work of Laban and his followers has amply displayed: the link with drama and dance is fundamental.

But the major creative medium is, of course, language—what David Holbrook has called 'the exploring word'.[2] Language is fundamental to human development—children without the necessary concepts lack the basic means to intellectual and emotional development. Language is expressive of emotion as well as an instrument of cognition; and the formulation of states of feeling in words is one of the major ways through which they can express and come to terms with the incoherence of their developing psyches.

The role of the teacher

Creative work, in this sense of disciplined attention, then, should form part of the educational diet of every child: and it is part of the job of the teacher to sensitise himself to the creative arts so that he can perform a delicate, but necessary, critical function in the lives of the children. Tact is always necessary, of course; and the teacher must learn when to interfere and how much. Often he will leave alone; but there are times when he must play the part of a more mature artist's own critical sense and ask whether what was meant to be said has actually been communicated. Only in this way can children be helped to grow beyond their present limits; after all, even an established artist must face his critics. A healthy state of critical reaction is a necessary ingredient in all true creativity: to have demands made or implied is itself part of the limitation making for a juster emotional response.

The role of the school

Yet the conditions for true creativity are not propitious;

G   81 there are not enough teachers with the necessary sensitivity to play the sort of delicate role implied. There is so little help from the environment; not only is there the lying degradation of popular culture to be lived through, but the traditions of high culture are themselves in danger of distintegration. High culture is now excessively cerebral (like a good deal of modern music and some types of painting) or excessively emotional (like action painting) or else obsessively concentrated on the contemporary, the new, even the momentary, chance collocation—the 'happening' (usually arranged). There is no longer a continuity but only a series of fashions; and the greatest artists have recognised in the break-down of continuity a desiccation and a loss. Let Picasso speak for many others:

But as soon as art had lost all link with tradition, and the kind of liberation that came in with Impressionism permitted every painter to do what he wanted to do, painting was finished. When they decided it was the painter's sensations and emotions that mattered, and every man could re-create painting as he understood it from any basis whatever, then there was no more painting; there were only individuals. Sculpture died the same death

Beginning with Van Gogh, however great we may be, we are all, in a measure, autodidacts—you might almost say primitive painters. Painters no longer live within a tradition and so each one of us must re-create an entire language. Every painter of our times is fully authorised to re-create that language from A to Z. No criterion can be applied to him *a priori*, since we don't believe in rigid standards any longer. In a certain sense, that's a liberation but at the same time it's an enormous limitation, because when the individuality of the artist begins to express itself, what the artist gains in the way of liberty he loses in the way of order, and when you're no longer able to attach yourself to an order, basically that's very bad.[3]

It is here, paradoxically, that the school could play a part; for if it will only avoid the temptation of taking the easy way out by stressing the contemporary, it can stand as a conservative force (literally conserving) in a disintegrating world. The dilemma arises out of the fact that the school-child has not only much to learn—he has so much to un-learn: the emotional falseness of popular culture. But he is to be taught by people who are themselves tempted by similar falsenesses and some of whom, inevitably, succumb.

Then, at the moment when one emphasises most the role of the school as a conservative force, one also appreciates the need for a profounder contemporaneity in the school. I don't mean that teachers should follow the superficial fashions of the hour, or encourage their pupils to be 'with it'. I do mean that they should try to grasp the significance of modernity, to understand the 'form' of the present, as Picasso, despite his pessimism, may nevertheless be said to have grasped the significance of our present phase of civilisation. It is here that an understanding of the past is most valuable as a perspective from which to realise the difference of the present; and perhaps, from such a perspective, the present will seem less insistently right than its more superficial exponents think of it as being. What is so frightening about so much of modern high culture is its unbelievable parochialism. And yet again, Picasso sees the folly of re-acting too strongly against the spirit of one's age: '. . . even if you are against a movement, you're still part of it. The pro and the con are, after all, two aspects of the same movement. In that way those of us who attempted to escape from Modern-Style became more Modern-Style than

83

anybody else. You can't escape your own period. Whether you take sides for or against, you're always inside it.'

So, ultimately, we must strive to understand our times as an inescapable part of the texture of our lives; and while historical perspective will reduce the arrogance, we must face our present problems and see in them the true challenge to education. And this means assessing the development of the modern consciousness. There seem to me to be three major influences affecting its progress; the mass media, the changed pattern of work and leisure, and the decay of authority, placing an increasing emphasis on personal decision-making. I will comment briefly on each in turn.

Freedom in the school

I have already commented on the decline in the extent of mythical understanding, traditionally the great source of authoritative beliefs and the pedagogic images based on them; so that, in a sinful world, at least people knew what was right and what was wrong. But the development of organised science, the scepticism inherent in the make-up of science (which must be always ready to reconstruct its beliefs, to alter its hypotheses) which has been accompanied by the break-down of old ethical and political absolutes and the extension of political participation to the whole population have necessitated a much deepened sense of *personal* decision-making and personal acceptance of responsibility. The schools must play their part in fostering this: they must face children with the need to make decisions relevant to their school life—but only as the children come to be able to appreciate the stakes at issue. Very young children have not sufficiently developed their understanding of moral concepts (as Piaget realised) to be afforded much freedom of choice: paradoxically, they need to accept the rightness or wrongness of actions before they come to a position when they are able to question decisions made on the basis of such moral assumptions. Too great a freedom of choice at too early an age is disintegrating to young children, who need the security of a firm framework within which to operate (as well as the teacher's superior judgment of what will serve their ultimate good). They can express likes and preferences but the teacher needs to judge the seriousness of the expression, as well as its function in the wise development of the child's intellectual and emotional powers. Often children have to do things on the basis of the teacher's authority (because the teacher is *an* authority as well as *in* authority) because the implication of participating or not participating are beyond the ability of the child to grasp at this stage.

Gradually, however, he will come to see the issues at stake in making a choice; and the teacher should never be so authoritarian that he does not see that he is looking forward to a time when children will no longer have the guidance of the school and will have to decide on their own volition. This means adopting two approaches to the subject of decision-making. Gradually children can be allowed more and more participation in school decisions relevant to their work and play—express opinions on their reactions to works of literature, choose, within reason, activities they would like to participate in, be given *reasons* for what they are doing. Then, also, they need to be given information which will help them make up their minds in matters relevant to their daily lives once they have left school—decisions relevant to home-making and general participation in the life of their communities, especially where children are going to leave school at 15. The domestic life is one of the centres round which the education of less able children should be centred—what to buy, how to cope with the baby and so on. It is out of the concrete situations with which they are faced that responsible decision-making can evolve, not out of abstract socio-political decisions about the atom bomb, the common market, capital punishment and the like of which the children have no direct experience and are unlikely to have the necessary information on which to form an intelligent judgment either now or, perhaps, ever. The Consumers' Association magazine, *Which*, can play a far greater role in promoting wise living, than any amount of abstract talk about democracy.

New cultural opportunities

The changed pattern of work and leisure will undoubtedly affect educational demand in several ways. There is the obvious point that, as automation develops, we shall need more technicians and machine-minders. This has, by now, been sufficiently hammered home. More fundamental are the implications of industrial development for the pattern of people's lives. The working week will undoubtedly decline and people will be faced with the problem of increased leisure. One response is the second job; another is the more creative use of leisure. People are used to treating work seriously; there is a long puritan tradition of labouring in one's vocation, and, in any case, there is the economic necessity. How will people face up to the possibilities of affluence and increased leisure? Can the schools do anything to deepen interests so that children are not let adrift in the new free time available, frittering it away among the pin-table or in the Bingo halls? The cultural opportunities are great, for, after all, a culture results from the unselfconscious participation of people in worthwhile activities which they pursue with discrimination and passion. *A*
86

cultivated person is not only a person who enjoys 'high' cultural activies based on the interests (literature, music, the arts and sciences) of the minority, but someone who is involved to the top of his ability in an activity with some width of perspective, such as gardening, still and moving photography, bird-watching, antique collecting, horse-riding, and a number of other pursuits and occupations, to the extent at least that he exploits the emotional, intellectual and practical possibilities inherent in them in a disciplined and organised way. It is through activities of this sort that we have the best chance of building up a genuine folk culture of the future. The tragedy implicit in the emphasis on the culture of literacy in our schools is not the inadequacy of that culture—it is one of the finest the world has seen—but its incompatibility with the potentialities of large numbers of people. A more thorough exploitation of genuine interests would show that many such people are not as stupid as school often seems to reveal, but are simply pursuing the wrong (for them) activities. For the Newsom child, at least, the traditional curriculum should be scrapped, and a wide range of activities with genuine cultural possibilities of a different kind in them substituted. (This, incidentally would also offer opportunities to teachers, many of whom are more bored with the traditional area of school subjects than they normally care to admit.)

Fundamental in any such reorientation of the school curriculum for the less able would be an attempt to meet the affective challenge of the mass media. This could be done by involving children much more in the arts and crafts (paint, pottery, wood and metal, drama and movement as well as language) as countervailing forces to the conventional passivity of media involvement. But the media also need to be investigated and utilised in their own terms.

Their social and psychological effects on the modern awareness are clearly profound—involving different sense perceptions and different possibilities of involvement from that offered by print. Their strongest cultural characteristic is probably that of actuality—they tailor the present for mass consumption. They capture (radio, TV and the reportage of the cinema) the fortuitous and the accidental, the transitory, the chance juxtaposition. They offer transitory participation in an immense range of life-styles. Their offerings are ephemeral (except when the tape-recorder, video or sound, intervenes) and their faults include those of superficiality and transcience. Yet, skilfully used, they can build up images—in sound or sight—which remain—and which educate. The modern world is inescapably involved in what Professor McLuhan has termed 'all-at-onceness'; but even the contemporary has depths which can be exploited and appreciated by *educated* minds.

So the school should learn to use the cinecamera, the tape-recorder, the TV and radio, not as aids which is what they are employed as at the moment, but as *cultural* media in all their affective potentialities. Film-making, script-writing, recording and editing have a place provided they are operated by trained teachers who have explored adequately the potentialities of the media.

The real issue in our times

For the ultimate battle between the school and the environment lies here. The school stands for depth, for order, for penetration. It is an institution set aside specifically for the purpose of introducing coherence and structure into what, in the outside world, is essentially inchoate and bewildering. Often it tries to do this with the wrong things for the pupils it has in mind, because it deals with sophisticated experiences beyond their present *and* future grasp. School, at present, provides a profound experience for the comparatively few. A little of its sophistication may rub off on to a further section of its pupils. But there are many whom it barely touches. And yet its concern for profundity was never more needed.

By contrast the environment affords rapidly changing, glibly superficial satisfactions, offerings of restless novelty, surface attractions which fail to feed the deep needs of young people growing up for stability as well as change, for coherence as well as variety. Apart from the *content* of what is offered, there is the sheer *volume* of disparate experience. The hard discreetness of personality is threatened by the ubiquity of transient impressions, meaningless juxtapositions: ' "Posters, shop windows, anything stuck on the walls all around us. I believe these images constitute *our* profundity," ' M. Alain Robbe-Grillet said recently in a newspaper interview. ' "The essence of modern man," he maintains, ". . . is no longer to be found within a hidden soul, but plastered on hoardings. . . . Therefore, study the surface, the object, for it contains the only answer." ' But, to the question as to whether he himself succeeds in being altogether this modern man, in rejecting the past for a life of surfaces and chance images, M. Robbe-Grillet admits his inability to dissolve into his surroundings: 'One is always a little nineteenth-century. I too have a soul, after all.'

Of course, we cannot avoid that awareness of our own position which is implicit in Robbe-Grillet's use of the word 'soul', with its overtones stretching back far into our history. In so far as the school feeds the soul, it is one of the few institutions in our society which give depth to the hoardings, the posters, the images moving and still our society restlessly feeds our young people. In doing so, it must realise that its function is both literate and post-literate: it must choose, as its vehicle, those modes of communication which are best suited to the immensely varying capacities of its youthful audience. Only in this way can school become at once a living experience and also feed the soul against the siren voices of distraction and fashion by which it is surrounded.

Notes

This is a small book on an immense topic. The student is strongly urged to follow up what is written here by consulting many of the books referred to in the notes. These notes are related to the text, so that particular points made briefly in the body of the book can be amplified by further study.

Chapter 1

1. There is an extensive literature on various aspects of English folk culture. Some of the best understanding is to be found in the works of imaginative writers who have appreciated the strength of the old rural culture without sentimentalising it or disguising its shortcomings: W. Cobbett: *Rural Rides*; *The Progress of a Ploughboy*; R. Jefferies: *Hodge and his Masters*; The Novels of Thomas Hardy; George Bourne (real name Sturt): *Change in the Village* (Duckworth, 1920); *A Farmer's Life* (Cape, 1922); *The Wheelwright's Shop* (Cambridge University Press, 1923); W. Rose: *The Village Carpenter* (Cambridge University Press, 1937); D. Kennedy: *England's Dances* (Bell, 1950); C. J. Sharp and others: *The Country Dance Book* (in six parts published by Novello between 1909 and 1922); G. E. Evans: *The Horse in the Furrow* (Faber, 1960); W. Muir: *Living with Balads* (Hogarth Press, 1965); J. and A. Lomax: *American Ballads and Folk Songs* (Macmillan, 1964); M. Lambert and E. Marx: *English Popular Art* (Batsford, 1951); P. Laslett: *The World we have lost* (Methuen, 1965); J. Reeves: *The Idiom of the People* (Heinemann, 1958); A. L. Lloyd: *The Singing Englishman* (Workers' Music Association); C. M. Bowra: *Primitive Song*

(Weidenfeld and Nicolson, 1962); E. P. Thompson: *The Making of the English Working Class* (Gollancz, 1963); E. W. Martin: *The Secret People* (Phoenix House, 1954); M. D. George: *England in Transition* (Routledge, 1931); J. L. and B. Hammond: *The Village Labourer* (Longmans, 1911); *The Skilled Labourer* (Longmans, 1919) A. L. Lloyd: *Folk Song in England* (Wishart, 1967).

2. L. C. Knights: 'Literature and the Study of Society' (University of Sheffield, 1947); J. M. Synge: *Plays* (Allen and Unwin, 1932); A. L. Rowse: *A Cornish Childhood* (Jonathan Cape, 1942).

3. By and large this did not survive, among the folk, the urbaniza-tion which followed the Industrial Revolution: 'What the urban-ization of the Industrial Revolution meant was the destruction of the older forms of community, in many cases rapidly, and in particular the destruction of those features of them to which religion had given symbolic expression.' [A. MacIntyre: *Secular-ization and Moral Change* (Oxford University Press, 1967.)]

4. On the significance of modern working conditions of Daniel Bell: *The End of Ideology* (New York: Free Press of Glencoe, 1962); R. S. and H. M. Lynd: *Middletown* (Constable, 1929); G. Friedmann: *Industrial Society* (New York: Free Press of Glencoe, 1955); *The Anatomy of Work* (Heinemann, 1962); Graham Turner: *The Car Makers* (Penguin, 1964).

5. On the growth of urbanisation cf. the works of Lewis Mumford: *The Culture of Cities* (Pelican, 1964); *Technics and Civilisation* (New York: Harcourt, Brace and Co., 1934); G. Sjoberg: *The Pre-Industrial City* (New York: Free Press of Glencoe, 1960).

6. Cf. Irving Howe: 'Notes on Mass Culture' in *Mass Culture*, ed. B. Rosenberg and D. M. White: '. . . mass culture must . . . not subvert the basic patterns of industrial life. It must provide relief from work monotony without making the return to work too unbearable; it must provide amusement without insight and pleasure without disturbance . . .'

7. George Bourne: *Change in the Village* (Duckworth, 1920).

8. A fuller treatment of what is said here will be found in G. H. Bantock: *Education in an Industrial Society* (Faber, 1963) [especially Chapter 7]; *Education, Culture and the Emotions* (Faber, 1967) [especially Chapter 5].

9. Some of the writings of D. H. Lawrence are of great educational interest. Cf. 'The Education of the People' (reprinted in *Phoenix*) and *Fantasia of the Unconscious*. The works of Lawrence are published by Heinemann. For a comment on Lawrence as educationist, cf. G. H. Bantock: *Freedom and Authority in Education*, Chapter 6 (Faber, 1965). For an account of his work as a teacher cf. L. Spolton: 'D. H. Lawrence—Student and Teacher' in *British Journal of Educational Studies*, Vol. XIV, No. 3, November, 1966. There are interesting passages on teaching in *Women in Love* and in the *Collected Poems*.

10. Cf. Nietzsche: *The Birth of Tragedy*.

11. On the press the following books are relevant: Francis Williams: *Dangerous Estate* (Longmans Green and Co., 1957); Denys Thompson: *Between the Lines* (Muller, 1939); *Royal Commission on the Press* (1947–1949), H.M.S.O.; R. Pound and G. Hainsworth: *Northcliffe* (Cassell, 1959); Tom Clarke: *My Northcliffe Diary* (Gollancz, 1931); E. W. Hildick: *A Close Look at Newspapers* (Faber, 1966); Norman Angell: *The Press and the Organisation of Society* (Gordon Fraser, Minority Press, 1932).

12. Cf. Marshall McLuhan: *Understanding Media* (Routledge and Kegan Paul, 1964).
On the various media, cf.:
(1) *Cinema:* S. Kracauer: *Nature of Film* (Dobson, 1961); H. Powdermaker: *Hollywood, The Dream Factory* (Little, Brown and Co., 1951); J. P. Mayer: *British Cinemas and their Audiences* (Dobson, 1948); *Sociology of Film* (Faber, 1946).
(2) *Television: Report of the Committee on Broadcasting*, 1960 (Pilkington Committee, H.M.S.O., 1962); Lyle, Schramm and Parker: *Television in the Lives of our children* (Oxford University Press, 1961).

Chapter 2

1. Relevant to an understanding of progressive ideas are: Rousseau: *Emile*; Froebel: *The Education of Man*; John Dewey: *School and Society*; *Democracy and Education*; Susan Isaacs: *The Children we Teach* (University of London, 1932); *Intellectual Development of Young Children* (Routledge and Kegan Paul, 1950).
For criticisms of progressive theory, cf. John Dewey: *Education and Experience*; I. B. Kandel:*The Cult of Uncertainty*; G. H. Bantock: *Freedom and Authority in Education*.

2. Cf. R. J. Montgomery: *Examinations* (Longmans, 1965); ed. S. Wiseman: *Examinations and English Education* (Manchester University Press, 1961).

3. Cf. R. King: 'Grammar School Values' (*New Society*, July 1st, 1965):
'. . . it is possible that the English Grammar School as a liberal cultural influence will be found to be as relatively ineffective as the American liberal arts colleges are suggested to be in the study of Jacob.' (P. E. Jacob: *Changing Values in College*, 1957.)

4. Cf. also J. F. Eggleston: *A Critical Review of Assessment Procedures in Secondary School Science* (University of Leicester, 1965).

5. May 14th, 1964; cf. also H. L. Wilensky: 'Mass Society and Mass Culture: interdependence or independence?' *American Sociological Review*, Vol. 29, No. 2, April, 1964.

6. This bears out, too uncomfortably for some, T. S. Eliot's thesis in *Notes Towards the Definition of Culture* concerning the importance of a hereditary element in the continuity of a nation's high culture.

7. Mark Pattison noted the same phenomenon even earlier, cf. J. Sparrow: *Mark Pattison and the Idea of a University* (Cambridge University Press, 1967).

8. Cf. P. Marris: *The Experience of Higher Education* (Routledge and Kegan Paul, 1964).

9. Sociological research seems to show that educational level of attainment in conventional terms (i.e. the possession of qualifications) is not an adequate predictor of behaviour *vis-à-vis* the media. As Mr. D. McQuail, in a paper to the British Sociological Association Conference in April, 1967, points out: 'education affects verbal statements of preference, but not actual behaviour'. And H. L. Wilensky (cf. Note 5) concludes, on the basis of a large-scale investigation, that 'educated strata—even products of graduate and professional schools—are becoming full participants in mass culture; they spend a reduced fraction of time in exposure to quality print and film. This trend extends to the professors, writers, artists, scientists—the keepers of high culture themselves'. It has been estimated that the average adult, with nine and a half waking hours at his disposal at home

on average daily, spends more time on watching TV than on any other single occupation—about 25 per cent of the total—2 hours and 25 minutes. The same survey assigned only 15 minutes a day to 'handicrafts, hobbies, study and gardening, with reading taking up 30 minutes'. Cf. M. Abrams: *The Newspaper Reading Public of Tomorrow* (Odhams, 1964).

Chapter 3

1. A small selection of the considerable literature on the theme is all that is possible here: T. S. Eliot: *Notes towards the Definition of Culture* (Faber, 1948); F. R. Leavis and Denys Thompson: *Culture and Environment* (Chatto and Windus, 1933); Denis de Rougemont: *Passion and Society* (Faber, 1962); *Popular Culture and Personal Responsibility* (N.U.T., 1960); Richard Hoggart: *The Uses of Literacy* (Chatto and Windus, 1957; Penguin, 1958); James D. Halloran: *Control or Consent?* (Sheed and Ward, 1963); B. Rosenberg and D. M. White (ed.): *Mass Culture* (New York: Free Press of Glencoe and Falcon's Wing Press, 1950); Norman Jacobs (ed.): *Culture for the Millions* (New York: Van Nostrand, 1961); Dwight MacDonald: *Against the American Grain* (Gallancz, 1963); Ortega y Gasset: *The Revolt of the Masses* (Allen and Unwin, 1932; Unwin Books, 1961); David Riesman (with Nathan Glazer and Reuel Denny): *The Lonely Crowd* (Yale University Press, 1950; Anchor Paperback, 1953); Marshall McLuhan: *The Gutenberg Galaxy* (Routledge and Kegan Paul, 1962); David Riesman: *Abundance for What?* (Chatto and Windus, 1964); Jacques Barzun: *The House of Intellect* (Secker and Warburg, 1959; Mercury paperback, 1962); David Holbrook: *The Secret Places* (Methuen, 1964); Denys Thompson: *Discrimination and Popular Culture* (Penguin, 1964); Leo Lowenthal: *Literature, Popular Culture and Society* (New Jersey: Prentice Hall, Spectrum Paperback, 1961); Q. D. Leavis: *Fiction and the Reading Public* (Chatto and Windus, 1932); Frederic Wertham: *Seduction of the Innocent* (Museum Press, 1956); George Orwell: *Critical Essays* (Secker and Warburg, 1951) and, also, the publications of the Centre for Contemporary Cultural Studies, University of Birmingham.

2. The work of Professor Marshall McLuhan is very relevant to the theme of this book. Cf. *The Mechanical Bride* (Routledge and Kegan Paul, 1967); *The Gutenberg Galaxy* (Routledge and Kegan Paul, 1962); *Understanding Media* (Routledge and Kegan Paul, 1964). A good introduction to his work is provided by R.

Kostelanetz: 'Marshall McLuhan' (*Twentieth Century*, Autumn, 1966).

3. D. Lerner: *The Passing of Traditional Society* (New York: Free Press of Glencoe, 1964).

4. Cf. C. Lévi-Strauss: *The Savage Mind* (Weidenfeld and Nicholson, 1966).

5. D. J. Boorstin: *The Image* (Penguin, 1963). This book contains an outstandingly good bibliography of the American literature.

6. Mircea Eliade: *Myth and Reality* (Allen and Unwin, 1964); Ernst Cassirer: *Language and Myth* (New York: Dover, 1946).

7. On advertising, cf. Denys Thompson: *The Voice of Civilisation* (Muller, 1943); M. Mayer: *Madison Avenue, U.S.A.* (Penguin, 1961); Vance Packard: *The Hidden Persuaders* (Penguin, 1960).

8. In the field of morals the objective case is well and clearly argued in S. E. Toulmin: *The Place of Reason in Ethics* (Cambridge University Press, 1950).

9. A good analysis of the role of 'fun' is to be found in Jules Henry: *Man Against Culture* (Tavistock, 1966).

10. Cf. J. D. Halloran: *The Effects of Mass Communication* (Leicester University Press, 1964); *Attitudes* (Leicester University Press, 1966); J. T. Klapper: *The Effects of Mass Communication* (New York Free Press of Glencoe, 1961).

11. Cf. a discussion by M. Jahoda and N. Warren in a review article, *Sociology of Education*, Winter, 1965.

Chapter 4

1. For a fuller account of the education of the emotions cf. G. H. Bantock: *Education, Culture and the Emotions* (Faber, 1967).

2. The works of David Holbrook are highly relevant to the theme of this book. The reader is especially recommended to consult *The Secret Places* (Methuen, 1964), *The Quest for Love* (Methuen, 1964) and *The Exploring Word* (Cambridge University Press 1967).

3. F. Gilot and C. Lake: *Life with Picasso* (Penguin, 1966).